MODERNIZING LOCAL GOVERNMENT TAXATION IN INDONESIA

APRIL 2022

ASIAN DEVELOPMENT BANK

© 2022 Asian Development Bank
6 ADB Avenue, Mandaluyong City, 1550 Metro Manila, Philippines
Tel +63 2 8632 4444; Fax +63 2 8636 2444
www.adb.org

Some rights reserved. Published in 2022.

ISBN 978-92-9269-453-1 (print); 978-92-9269-454-8 (electronic); 978-92-9269-455-5 (ebook)
Publication Stock No. TCS220138-2
DOI: http://dx.doi.org/10.22617/TCS220138-2

The views expressed in this publication are those of the authors and do not necessarily reflect the views and policies of the Asian Development Bank (ADB) or its Board of Governors or the governments they represent.

ADB does not guarantee the accuracy of the data included in this publication and accepts no responsibility for any consequence of their use. The mention of specific companies or products of manufacturers does not imply that they are endorsed or recommended by ADB in preference to others of a similar nature that are not mentioned.

By making any designation of or reference to a particular territory or geographic area, or by using the term "country" in this document, ADB does not intend to make any judgments as to the legal or other status of any territory or area.

Corrigenda to ADB publications may be found at http://www.adb.org/publications/corrigenda.

Note:
In this publication, "$" refers to United States dollars.

On the cover: Property tax is a principal means by which local governments raise local-source tax revenue. Thus, upgrading the property tax administration through fiscal cadastre updating is the key support of the Asian Development Bank under the Tax Revenue Administration Modernization and Policy Improvement in Local Governments (TRAMPIL) project.

Cover design by PT Cartenz Technology Indonesia.

CONTENTS

TABLES, FIGURES, AND BOXES

FOREWORD

As Indonesia embarks on the challenging process of recovering from the impacts of the coronavirus disease (COVID-19) pandemic, the role of local governments in ensuring that public goods and services are delivered to Indonesians in every corner of the archipelago will become even more critical.

Integral to the fulfillment of this mandate is the need to improve the capacity of local governments to generate tax revenue from local sources. Even prior to the pandemic, a third of all local government units in the country were only able to finance 5% of their budgets with locally sourced revenue. The need to increase this ratio is even more apparent given the central government's desire to reduce pressure on its fiscal balance.

In line with the thrust of the Asian Development Bank (ADB) to support inclusive and sustainable development in Indonesia, it carried out the Tax Revenue Administration Modernization and Policy Improvement in Local Governments (TRAMPIL) technical assistance project from 2015 to 2020. Over 6 years, the TRAMPIL project analyzed the challenges in raising local tax revenue, worked with the Ministry of Finance on needed regulatory amendments, and tested several strategies to modernize tax administrations in four pilot areas: Badung, Bali; Balikpapan, East Kalimantan; Bandung, West Java; and the Special Capital Region (DKI) of Jakarta.

The results are extremely encouraging. With improved tax administration processes, the pilot local governments were able to increase their local tax collections by an average of almost 37% from 2015 to 2018. Efforts to simplify the tax administration system, for instance, not only improved collection efficiency, but also the ease of doing business and tax compliance. The gains made and lessons learned through TRAMPIL, as outlined in this report, show viable solutions that other local governments across the country can adopt.

With regional autonomy embedded in Indonesia's legal, social, and political fabric, it is imperative that local governments be equipped with sufficient capacity to manage their own fiscal and development affairs. ADB is committed to continuing its strong support to the Government of Indonesia and local governments in rolling out state-of-the-art local government tax systems, toward the ultimate goal of improving the welfare of regional economies and the people of Indonesia.

Winfried F. Wicklein
Deputy Director General
Southeast Asia Department
Asian Development Bank

PREFACE

The purpose of this report is to help local governments in Indonesia increase their local-source tax revenue. This objective is accomplished through a review of the achievements and challenges of the Tax Revenue Administration Modernization and Policy Improvement in Local Governments (TRAMPIL) project of the Asian Development Bank (ADB) which operated in Indonesia from 2015 to 2020, and through recommendations of avenues for further progress. Accordingly, the report draws on the analysis and operations carried out by TRAMPIL.

The devolution of local government revenue-raising in Indonesia must be addressed in the context of the country's constitutionally mandated regional autonomy and the statutory prerequisite that the central government alone is responsible for managing the fiscal and monetary policy of Indonesia as a unitary state. Consequently, local governments do not have unfettered rights to impose taxes unilaterally in whatever manner they see fit. It is within this framework that the report addresses the recent achievements of Indonesia's local governments in their quest for greater local-source revenue mobilization and the challenges they continue to face, which will determine the extent that new local government tax initiatives can be developed in the future.

TRAMPIL was implemented before the coronavirus disease (COVID-19) pandemic hit, which has created global economic uncertainty. TRAMPIL was also implemented before the Law of 1/2022 on Financial Relation Between Central and Local Government was approved by the Parliament in December 2021. For Indonesia alone, an unprecedented economic crisis brought on a real gross domestic product contraction of more than 5% in 2020. In response to the crisis, Indonesian tax authorities introduced fiscal stimuli while adjusting tax collection strategies, such as tax deferrals for a period of time without incurring penalties. Consequently, tax authorities faced significant revenue losses. Although this report is not intended to specifically address post-COVID-19 local tax policy and administration adaptation, the knowledge and operations that TRAMPIL introduced, which are presented in this knowledge report, are nevertheless highly relevant for local tax administration offices to modernize their tax administration. In this way, when the economy recovers, local tax offices will be ready for better tax data integration to enable better tax services and collection.

To establish the macroeconomic context, Chapter 1 presents a brief outline of the aspects of central government fiscal policies that are relevant to local government revenue generation. Chapter 2 considers the historical course of constitutional and other statutory developments concerning regional autonomy and the sources of finance. That history demonstrates the tension between the drive for regional autonomy and the central government's control of the overall economy of Indonesia.

At the broad policy level, Chapter 3 offers a synopsis of policy proposals suggested by TRAMPIL and certain aspects of the proposed amendments to Law No. 28 of 2009 concerning local taxes and charges, which was being discussed at the inter-ministerial level during the period of TRAMPIL implementation.

At the micro level, Chapter 3 discusses TRAMPIL achievements in four pilot local government tax administrations, the obstacles that TRAMPIL faced during the 5-year period of technical assistance, and the challenges confronting local governments as they proceed with local-source revenue generation in the future. Chapter 3 offers recommendations on how to meet those challenges.

Chapter 4 addresses a selection of deeper policy issues considered primarily to broaden the local government revenue base over the long term, and Chapter 5 recommends how to progress from the current state of affairs. A local government tax administration model is presented, and observed variance from it in the pilot local governments is described to identify the areas of local government tax administration that require immediate attention. The analysis culminates in a set of minimum common standards for adoption by all local government tax administrations in Indonesia, to ensure that reform proceeds in a sustainable and reasonably uniform manner.

Against this backdrop, Chapter 5 presents four options on how to advance local government revenue mobilization following the end of the TRAMPIL technical assistance. More broadly, the report advocates a greater role for the Directorate General of Fiscal Balance and for other directorates of the Ministry of Finance in local government tax reform and, due to the impact of reform on other arms of government, increased coordination and strategy formulation across ministries.

Jakarta, 17 December 2020

ACKNOWLEDGMENTS

This report is a collaborative work under the capacity development technical assistance (CDTA) of the Asian Development Bank (ADB) through the Tax Revenue Administration Modernization and Policy Improvement in Local Governments (TRAMPIL) project, generously cofinanced by the Government of Switzerland's State Secretariat for Economic Affairs. Drawing from the operational experience of implementing the CDTA, this report presents knowledge and practical insights to inform stakeholders in policy and administration modernization on domestic resource mobilization. Publication of this report was sponsored by the ADB Domestic Resource Mobilization Trust Fund, with contribution from the Government of Japan.

We thank the Directorate General of Fiscal Balance at the Ministry of Finance of the Republic of Indonesia, DKI Jakarta Revenue Agency (Bapenda), Bapenda Badung, Bandung Revenue Management Agency, and Balikpapan Tax and Retribution Management Agency for their strong engagement and cooperation alongside the technical assistance implementation that steered the analysis of the report.

We also thank Kevin Holmes, Paul Tambunan, and Gito Wahyudi for supporting the drafting of the report; Yurendra Basnett for overall strategy and guidance; PT Cartenz Technology Indonesia and team for the initial graphics and layout design; and Anna Rini Hariandja and Dewi Kahulunan for administrative support. The report benefited from the external peer reviewers who provided inputs and comments to strengthen the quality of the report, Riatu M. Qibthiyyah and B. Raksaka Mahi of the Institute for Economic and Social Research of the University of Indonesia, as well as our internal peer reviewer, Aekapol Chongvilaivan. Peter Fredenburg, Joanne G. Elayne, and Hannah Maddison-Harris provided editorial support; Alvin Tubio provided typesetting; Corazon Desuasido proofread; and Ma. Cecilia Abellar provided page-proof checking.

We express our appreciation to Winfried Wicklein, deputy director general of the Southeast Asia Department, and Said Zaidansyah, deputy country director of the Indonesia Resident Mission, for their support and guidance in finalizing this knowledge report.

Deeny Simanjuntak
Senior Project Officer and Task Team Leader

ABBREVIATIONS

ADB	Asian Development Bank
BPHTB	*bea pengalihan hak atas tanah dan bangunan* (duty on the acquisition of land and building rights)
CMEA	Coordinating Ministry for Economic Affairs
COVID-19	coronavirus disease
DAK	*dana alokasi khusus* (special allocation fund)
DAU	*dana alokasi umum* (general allocation fund)
DBH	*dana bagi hasil* (revenue sharing fund)
DGFB	Direktorat Jenderal Perimbangan Keuangan (Directorate General of Fiscal Balance)
DGT	Directorate General of Taxation
DID	*dana insentif daerah* (regional incentive fund)
DKI Jakarta	Daerah Khusus Ibukota (Special Capital Region) of Jakarta
GDP	gross domestic product
GPS	global positioning system
ICT	information and communication technology
IMF	International Monetary Fund
IT	information technology
LTA	local tax administration
LTO	large taxpayer office
MOF	Ministry of Finance
MOHA	Kementerian Dalam Negeri (Ministry of Home Affairs)
MTO	medium-sized taxpayer office
NJOP	*nilai jual objek pajak* (tax object sales value)
OECD	Organisation for Economic Co-operation and Development
PAD	*pendapatan asli daerah* (locally generated revenue)
PBB-P2	*pajak bumi dan bangunan perdesaan dan perkotaan* (urban and rural land and building tax)
PBB-P3	*pajak bumi dan bangunan pertambangan, perhutanan dan perkebunan* (land and building tax for mining, forestry, and plantations)
PIT	personal income tax

SIKAP   Standar Indikator Kinerja Administrasi Pajak Daerah
             (Performance Indicator Standard for Local Tax Administration)

SISMIOP   Sistem Manajemen Informasi Objek Pajak
             (Tax Object Information Management System)

TRAMPIL   Tax Revenue Administration Modernization and Policy Improvement
             in Local Governments

VAT   value-added tax

CURRENCY EQUIVALENTS

(as of 31 December 2020)

Currency unit   –   rupiah (Rp)

Rp10,000   = $0.70896

$1.00   =   Rp14,105

TRAMPIL

Tax Revenue Administration Modernization and Policy Improvement in Local Governments (TRAMPIL) was a $5 million technical assistance project cofinanced by the Asian Development Bank (ADB) and the Government of Switzerland's State Secretariat for Economic Affairs. It was administered by ADB as part of its support for the strengthening of local governance, particularly in revenue administration. TRAMPIL commenced on 4 May 2015 and terminated on 30 April 2020.

TRAMPIL supported the Government of Indonesia in strengthening local tax revenue policy and administration at both the central and local levels of government, in line with the government's national strategy to increase the ratio of local tax revenue to gross domestic product from 1.7% in 2015 to 1.9% in 2018.

The Directorate General of Fiscal Balance (DGFB), under the Ministry of Finance (MOF), was the executing agency, and the Directorate of Regional Financial Revenue and Capacity was the implementing agency for national activities. The governments of the Special Capital Region (DKI) of Jakarta, the cities of Bandung and Balikpapan, and the district of Badung—each represented by a local tax service unit—were selected as the pilot subnational implementing agencies.

At the central level, the focus was on developing policy-making capacity, improving the main regulatory framework for local revenue mobilization, and building DGFB capacity to effectively manage the devolution of certain taxes to local governments. TRAMPIL supported the MOF's efforts to strengthen Law No. 28 of 2009 concerning local taxes and charges, and its regulations on implementation. Policy formulation for this component of TRAMPIL was carried out by the Institute for Economic and Social Research of the University of Indonesia, in association with the Georgia State University Research Foundation in the United States.

At the local level, TRAMPIL focused on mobilizing local tax revenues and on supporting institutional and systems transformation to enable more modern, efficient, and credible revenue administration in the selected pilot local governments, which, despite their capacity deficiencies, have the potential to increase their local-source revenue. These activities helped the pilot local governments to expand their tax bases and taxpayer compliance. The tax administration modernization element of the project was implemented by PT Cartenz Technology Indonesia.

Modernizing Local Government Taxation in Indonesia

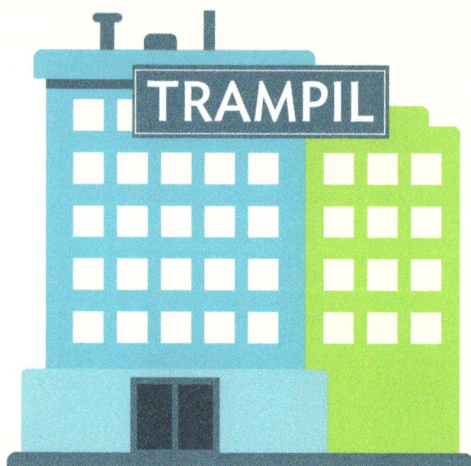

TRAMPIL

**Tax Revenue Administration Modernization
and Policy Improvement in Local Governments**

The Tax Revenue Administration Modernization and Policy Improvement
in Local Governments (TRAMPIL) technical assistance project aimed to
support the Government of Indonesia in its strengthening of local tax revenue
policy and administration at the central and local levels of government,
with the aim of increasing local-source tax revenue collections by
local governments.

Administered by

ADB ASIAN DEVELOPMENT BANK

Cofinanced by

Schweizerische Eidgenossenschaft
Confédération suisse
Confederazione Svizzera
Confederaziun svizra

Swiss Confederation

Federal Department of Economic Affairs,
Education and Research EAER
State Secretariat for Economic Affairs SECO

MACRO LEVEL

**TRAMPIL Policy Assistance to the
Directorate General of Fiscal Balance (DGFB)**

Suggested local government tax policy reforms
and proposed amendments to Law No. 28 of 2009
on local taxes and charges.

See Chapter 3 for details.

MICRO LEVEL

**TRAMPIL Implementation Assistance
to DGFB and Local Governments**

Worked with four pilot local governments to
modernize their local tax administration structures
and practices and to update their property tax
fiscal cadastres.

See Chapter 3 for details.

Directorate General of Fiscal Balance

The Directorate General of Fiscal Balance (DGFB) at the Ministry of Finance (MOF) was the executing agency, and the Directorate of Regional Financial Revenue and Capacity was the implementing agency for national-level activities.

MOVING FORWARD

Maximizing the Impact of TRAMPIL

This can be achieved by adopting minimum common standards and rolling out TRAMPIL outputs nationally. Knowledge management tools will play an important role in fostering the awareness and buy-in of local governments and other external stakeholders for local-source revenue mobilization.

See Chapters 4 and 5 for details.

TECHNICAL ASSISTANCE PROGRAM

TRAMPIL was a technical assistance project cofinanced by the Asian Development Bank (ADB) and the Government of Switzerland's State Secretariat for Economic Affairs, and administered by ADB. The project supported the Government of Indonesia in the strengthening of local tax revenue policy and administration at the central and local levels of government, in line with its national strategy of lifting the ratio of local tax revenue to gross domestic product.

Local-source revenue must be mobilized to provide a sustainable and independent source of income to local governments toward fulfilling a constitutional mandate for regional autonomy.

TRAMPIL provided technical assistance from 2015 to 2020 to counter the prevailing challenges to raising national tax revenue, and to support the central government's key economic policies of attracting more investment, improving the ease of doing business, and ultimately accelerating national economic growth.

The pace of reform was constrained, however, by vast divergences across Indonesia's 34 provinces in their economic performance and access to resources.

The DGFB of the MOF was the executing agency, and the Directorate of Regional Financial Revenue and Capacity was the implementing agency for national activities.

At the national level, the focus was on developing policy-making capacity, enhancing the main regulatory framework for local revenue mobilization, and building up the capacity of the DGFB to effectively manage the devolution of certain taxes to local governments. TRAMPIL supported the MOF in strengthening Law 28/2009 concerning local taxes and charges, and its implementing regulations.

At the local level, TRAMPIL focused on mobilizing local tax revenue and supporting institutional and system transformation to enable more modern, efficient, and credible revenue administration in selected pilot local governments.

The governments of the Special Capital Region of Jakarta, the cities of Bandung and Balikpapan, and the district of Badung—each represented by its local tax service unit—were selected as "pilot" implementing agencies at the subnational level.

Policy enhancement must operate in parallel with the modernization of local tax administrations (LTAs) to strengthen local-source tax-collection capacity, and thus afford local governments greater fiscal independence.

MACRO LEVEL

Policy proposals suggested by TRAMPIL, in collaboration with the DGFB, offered ways to broaden the local tax base to be included in the proposed amendments to Law 28/2009, concerning local taxes and charges.

TRAMPIL provided a broad range of advice to the DGFB on the formulation of policy pertaining to local government revenue-raising measures. Topics included

- local tax policy, revenue mobilization, and intergovernmental transfer policies, as well as the impact of devolution of land and building taxes from mining, forestry, and plantations (PBB-P3);
- simplified modeling of the sales value of tax objects (NJOP);
- local government business and income tax surcharges;
- policies on user charges;
- the choice between a value-added tax and retail sales tax to replace local sales taxes on services;
- models for revenue sharing between provinces and their districts and cities, to minimize manipulation by provincial governments;
- local government "piggybacking" on national taxes;
- tobacco excise taxes;
- taxes on motor vehicles; and
- taxes on water extraction.

TRAMPIL assisted the MOF with amendments to Law 28/2009 to broaden the tax base, increase tax rates, and rationalize tax administration burdens.

TRAMPIL assisted the DGFB in drafting much-needed improvements to Law 28/2009.

Chapter 3

MICRO LEVEL

TRAMPIL scored significant achievements in four pilot LTAs, despite a number of obstacles that it faced during the 5 years of technical assistance, as well as the challenges that continue to confront local governments as they proceed with local-source revenue generation in the future.

- The TRAMPIL work with the pilot local governments showed that substantial local tax revenue gains can be achieved by upgrading LTA systems and procedures.
- However, LTAs face capacity deficits as follows:
  ☐ human resource capacity limitations,
  ☐ a lack of comprehensive fiscal cadastre databases,
  ☐ information technology deficiencies, and
  ☐ barriers to efficient taxpayer compliance.

- Commitment to tackling these deficiencies varies among local governments and within them.
- Human capacity limitations in LTAs arise from the inability of many regions to attract suitably qualified staff and from very frequent and uncoordinated staff rotation.
- Given the importance of property taxation as a local government revenue source, assistance in upgrading fiscal cadastres in pilot LTAs was a dominant feature of direct TRAMPIL support to local governments.
- Improvements in taxpayer compliance with local government self-assessment tax obligations can be achieved by
  ☐ enforcing better compliance with underlying regulatory obligations,
  ☐ boosting capacity to detect underreported revenue, especially through an enhanced coordination of audits and exchange of information with the Directorate General of Taxes, and
  ☐ introducing large taxpayer offices in the LTAs of bigger cities.
- The Performance Indicator Standard for Local Tax Administration diagnostic tool was developed to allow local governments to assess their tax administration performance and identify areas for improvement. This tool will sustain the impetus of TRAMPIL tax administration improvements.

TRAMPIL and the DGFB worked with four pilot local governments to implement TRAMPIL outputs. Updating tax object data in property tax fiscal cadastres was a key foundation for modernizing LTA. Other lessons were drawn from TRAMPIL advice on LTA structures and processes.

MOVING FORWARD

The following three broad recommendations aim to capitalize on the impact of TRAMPIL:
- Adopt common minimum tax administration standards across all local governments.
- Consider a range of deeper policy issues to expand the local government tax base over the long term.
- Develop a strategy to roll out LTA modernization, expanding from the four pilot local governments to the remaining local governments in a uniform and sustainable manner.

- Capture future policy development opportunities to broaden the local government tax base in the long term.
- Roll out minimum common standards across all LTAs to align them more closely with a "model" tax administration.
- Develop under the central government incentivization mechanisms to induce local governments to embark on tax reform.
- Follow a proposed four-tier reform pathway for the future that tackles both internal and external demands regarding tax policy formulation and tax administration as follows:
  ☐ **Tier 1:** Continue, at the LTA operational level, capacity development along the lines of activities undertaken in the pilot local governments by TRAMPIL.
  ☐ **Tier 2:** Expand capacity building at the next level to enhance the tax policy-making DGFB staff; broaden the involvement of the DGFB in the direction and supervision of the rollout of reform; and act as a catalyst for the dissemination of knowledge products to local governments, and facilitating change management as necessary.
  ☐ **Tier 3:** Adopt a "whole-of-government" approach that coordinates cooperation between the local governments and the relevant directorates of the MOF, and among the directorates themselves, particularly in the conduct of joint audits, exchange of information, and development of legislation founded on sound policy.
  ☐ **Tier 4:** Pursue a pan-ministry "holistic" approach to developing strategies to ensure that local government tax reforms that affect areas of government outside of local government taxation per se are properly addressed, and that reform is compatible with, or accommodated by, the policies and practices of those other areas of governance, to ensure that Indonesia as a whole is better off as a result of reform.

Rolling out TRAMPIL nationally will require a commitment from both the central government and local governments. The commitment of stakeholders beyond the DGFB and the local governments is vital to capture the benefits of TRAMPIL technical assistance, as is the dissemination of knowledge management tools.

EXECUTIVE SUMMARY

Regional autonomy, as mandated by the Indonesian Constitution, depends on the successful devolution of independent local-source revenue generation to local governments within macroeconomic parameters determined by the central government. Historically, local governments have relied on central government financial transfers, leaving them with little incentive to raise their own revenue. This report explains the problem and proposes how it can be successfully resolved. Policy makers are advised to heed the recommendations in this report if they want to ensure sustainable regional autonomy in Indonesia and move on from the existing uninspired approach to financing local government expenditure.

Indonesia is an emerging market economy of immense diversity with regard to its geography, culture, natural resource endowment, and economic activity. That diversity has generated regional inequalities, as illustrated by the broad range of per capita incomes across the country. One consequence of this disparity is the different needs for public goods and services in different regions, and another is the contrasting abilities of the regional governments to finance them. Regional autonomy in Indonesia is a deep-seated constitutional and political imperative. The successful devolution of powers to subnational governments requires them to obtain revenue to fund the expenditure needed to meet the needs of their regional populations. Historically, that income has primarily been allocated by the central government.

The central government now requires local governments to raise a greater portion of their revenue from local sources. By law, one of the seven responsibilities of the central government is to manage Indonesia's monetary and fiscal policy. In carrying out that responsibility, the central government needs to reduce pressure on its fiscal balance. One way to do this is for subnational governments to raise more local-source revenue to finance their expenditures, and thereby rely less on central government transfers. This policy also gives regional governments an incentive to become more accountable to their local communities.

When raising more local-source revenue, local governments must conform to central government macroeconomic objectives and policies. The pivotal policy objective is economic growth facilitated by increased investment and ease of doing business. Harnessing the full potential of sustainable economic development to achieve the central government's objectives requires the active participation of local governments, given the powers that they have inherited under Indonesia's decentralization laws and policies. It is within that broad framework that the Tax Revenue Administration Modernization and Policy Improvement in Local Governments (TRAMPIL) was carried out from 2015 to 2020, and the next phase of measures to increase local-source revenue must also be carried out within that framework, with external technical support.

Indonesia's experience in raising national tax revenue highlights a number of contextual challenges to raising local-source revenue. While the country has maintained positive economic growth since 2015, approximately 10% of the population lives below the national poverty line, with a further 20% only marginally above it. This excludes nearly one-third of the population from a viable tax base. The limited nature of the tax base is evidenced by Indonesia's low tax revenue collection. In 2018, the ratio of tax revenues to gross domestic product (GDP) was 11.5%, and in 2017, the ratio of personal income taxes to GDP was 0.9%.

Both figures rank Indonesia second to last in Southeast Asia. Indonesia's large informal sector keeps compliance low despite the legal tax liability in the sector. Low tax compliance is an obstacle confronting local governments in their quest to raise additional tax revenue in their jurisdictions.

TRAMPIL provided policy and administration technical assistance to support the drive to increase local government tax revenue. Policy advice was given to the Directorate General of Fiscal Balance (DGFB), the central government agency responsible for formulating and implementing local tax reform. Assistance in modernizing local tax administration was given to four pilot local governments. TRAMPIL's experiences with pilot local tax administrations (LTAs) provided insights to DGFB decision makers regarding a potential rollout of measures to enhance local-source tax revenue generation across all of Indonesia's local governments.

TRAMPIL was successful in both tax policy and tax implementation. At the policy level, TRAMPIL provided a broad range of advice to the DGFB on the formulation of measures to help local governments to raise revenue. This included analytical reports, policy briefs, and focus group discussions on

(i)   local tax policy, revenue mobilization, and intergovernmental transfer policies;

(ii)   the impact of devolution of land and building taxes from mining, forestry, and plantations;

(iii)   simplified modeling of the sales value of tax objects;

(iv)   local business and income tax surcharges;

(v)   policies on user charges;

(vi)   the choice between a value-added tax or retail sales tax to replace local sales taxes on services;

(vii)   models for revenue sharing between provinces and their districts and cities that would minimize manipulation by provincial governments;

(viii) local government piggybacking on national taxes;

(ix)   tobacco excise taxes;

(x)   motor vehicle taxation; and

(xi)   taxes on water extraction.

TRAMPIL assisted the Ministry of Finance (MOF) with amendments to Law 28/2009 concerning local taxes and charges. Key recommendations incorporated into the proposed amendments to the law are intended to broaden the tax base, increase tax rates, and rationalize tax administration burdens. However, these policy and legislative improvements did not gain much political traction, and the amending legislation has languished low in the National Legislation Program, having awaited debate since 2014.

A number of policy questions still call for deeper consideration. For example, further attention needs to be given to the following:

(i)   a better alignment of motor vehicle-related taxes with the benefit principle of taxation,

(ii)   the cascading effect of local government taxes on goods and services supplied to businesses,

(iii)   the manner in which exemptions to property taxes apply,

(iv) the economic efficiency effects of transfer taxes, and

(v) the propriety of piggybacking on personal income taxes.

Moreover, further thought was needed to find novel policies to broaden the local government tax base.
This occurred because nearly three-quarters of Indonesia's local governments already take advantage of most of the taxes available to them under the current law. Opportunities exist for local governments to broaden the application of existing taxes and to impose new taxes in line with the benefit principle of taxation, including

(i) tourism accommodation taxes beyond the current hotel tax,

(ii) environment and health-related behavioral taxes,

(iii) betterment taxes, and

(iv) local franchise fees.

The quality of policy decision-making depends on the reliable and timely reporting of data.
During TRAMPIL, it was observed that the central repository of local government revenue data was not adequately detailed or collated on a timely basis. These shortcomings revealed the need for a unified, properly integrated information and communication technology apparatus to record the receipt of each revenue type by each local government on a regular basis, ideally daily or in real time. Resolving this quality-of-data issue required central government intervention to stipulate the

(i) minimum common data recording standards,

(ii) uniform reporting formats, and

(iii) time limits for the submission of data.

For tax administration, the work of TRAMPIL in the pilot local governments showed where substantial local tax revenue gains were feasible. Existing law offered the means to bring local government tax administration systems and practices up to international standards. Nonetheless, local government tax administrations currently face a significant practical constraint in the form of a capacity deficit, which manifests itself in

(i) limitations in human resource capacity, notably for valuation, supervision, and audits;

(ii) a lack of comprehensive fiscal cadastre databases;[1]

(iii) information technology (IT) deficiencies; and

(iv) barriers to efficient taxpayer compliance.

Commitment to reforming the deficiencies varies among and within local governments.
Stakeholder resistance needs to be addressed by the central government, by maintaining communication and coordination with local governments to ensure their ongoing commitment to reform, and by enunciating the benefits of reform for their communities and for the local governments themselves.

---

[1] A cadastre is a "[l]ocal public registry where real property is recorded for purposes of value, ownership and transfers of the property..." and a fiscal cadastre is a cadastre compiled for taxation. IBFD–Tax Research Platform. International Tax Glossary. https://research.ibfd.org/#/glossary.

Furthermore, the higher tiers of local government must impress upon the lower tiers the importance of committing themselves to reform.

Human capacity limitations in LTAs arise from an inequality in the ability of different regions to attract suitably qualified staff, and from the very frequent and uncoordinated staff rotation. This inequality necessitates the introduction of incentives to attract skilled staff to less-appealing regions, excessive rotation requires a revision of staff-rotation policies, and both require the participation of the Ministry of Home Affairs, as they involve the terms of employee engagement.

TRAMPIL took steps to overcome these challenges. The technical assistance helped the pilot LTAs to improve the state of their fiscal cadastres, adopt function-based operational practices, implement more integrated IT systems, and enhance their tax collection methods. A range of draft guidelines and knowledge products were produced to buttress these improvements. The products, to be issued by the DGFB, include

(i)   a fiscal cadastre manual;

(ii)   a property valuation manual;

(iii)   a manual on the collection of tax payments in arrears, and a guide on general tax-collection methodology;

(iv)   a business process design manual;

(v)   guidelines on tax administration organizational structures;

(vi)   a human capital management and change-management manual;

(vii)   a taxpayer satisfaction survey manual;

(viii) an employee engagement survey manual;

(ix)   a concept note on monitoring and collecting taxes from tourist accommodation providers that use online reservation platforms;

(x)   IT blueprints;

(xi)   TRAMPIL website user manuals; and

(xii)   a diagnostic tool that provides a performance indicator standard for local tax administration.

Assistance in upgrading the pilot local governments' fiscal cadastres was central to the TRAMPIL project. This reflected the importance of property taxation to local government revenue. TRAMPIL support yielded substantial increases in the recorded number of tax objects and in the potential additional revenue from urban and rural land and building taxes. TRAMPIL assistance included training in comprehensive fiscal cadastre updating, from data collection planning through mapping and field surveys, and in quality control of the collected data.

TRAMPIL's work with the four pilot LTAs revealed a need for more sophisticated IT systems in local governments. Common shortcomings were weak data governance and the failure to integrate information systems into a single core IT system. To help the pilot local governments upgrade their IT systems, TRAMPIL developed medium-term IT blueprints, both general and specific, based on IT gap analyses, which generated recommendations on system design and road maps for implementation.

TRAMPIL supported the LTA of DKI Jakarta as it upgraded the integrity of its data governance by separating administrator and user functions.

Considerable scope exists for increasing taxpayer compliance with local government self-assessment tax obligations. Increased compliance can be achieved in three primary ways, as follows:

(i)   better compliance with underlying regulatory obligations through stricter enforcement of taxpayers' obligations to comply with nontax regulations that have tax consequences, such as obtaining permits to extract groundwater (which identifies a source of local government tax revenue in the groundwater tax, while illegal and undetected extraction of groundwater means lost tax revenue);

(ii)   improved capacity to detect underreported revenue, which is the basis for most self-assessment taxes, through the coordination of audits and information exchange with the Directorate General of Taxation; and

(iii)   the introduction of special offices devoted to large taxpayers in the LTAs of bigger cities.

Further, raising general tax-enforcement standards across local governments will enhance taxpayer compliance.

TRAMPIL carried out employee and taxpayer surveys in the pilot LTAs to help improve LTA service delivery. Employee engagement and perception surveys identified service delivery and IT systems as particularly in need of improvement. Businesses complained of poor comprehension by local tax personnel when dealing with their tax affairs, which points to a need for intensive training to lift staff technical expertise. Taxpayer satisfaction and perception surveys served as inputs for a taxpayer satisfaction index.

A dedicated TRAMPIL website was developed to facilitate the dissemination of TRAMPIL outputs. This was the first step toward sustaining the impetus of TRAMPIL tax administration improvements. It was proposed that the website would be hosted on the MOF server and administered by the DGFB. Local governments would choose knowledge products off the shelf and apply them in ways that are most appropriate for their individual circumstances. The website would also allow for bottom–up knowledge sharing, enabling local governments whose experiences in tax reform have generated appropriate solutions that could be useful to other local governments in similar circumstances.

This report presents a simplified 12-point tax-administration model for local governments. It will enable LTAs to conceptualize what they will need to achieve their local-source revenue mobilization objectives. Variance between the model and current practice in the pilot local governments was measured to identify which areas required more attention and capacity building, to enable LTAs to better emulate the tax administration model. This led, in turn, to the articulation of minimum common standards that the LTAs would need to adopt in order to instill the confidence, commitment, and operational capacity needed to carry out reform in a reasonably consistent manner across Indonesia.

The key areas of the tax administration model and minimum common standards cover the top-end management elements of (i) policy analysis, IT, and human resource management; (ii) accountability; and (iii) revenue management.

They also cover the following operational elements:

(i)   taxpayer services,

(ii)   registration databases,

(iii) the filing of self-assessment tax returns,

(iv)   official assessments,

(v)   the audit of self-assessment tax returns,

(vi)   the payment of taxes,

(vii) the collection and recovery of taxes,

(viii) offenses and penalties, and

(ix)   taxpayer dispute resolution.

The four pilot local governments improved their local-source tax revenue collection by almost 37% from 2015 to 2018. TRAMPIL technical assistance, which improved the tax administration processes in the pilot LTAs, contributed to this increased collection of tax revenue.

Local governments must have incentives to embark on local-source tax reform. The self-defeating danger to avoid is effectively penalizing local governments by reducing their revenue allocations from the central government once they start raising revenue of their own, on the grounds that the fiscal gaps to be filled by the revenue allocations become smaller, given the increase in locally raised revenue.

This problem should be addressed by introducing

(i)   special funding measures to compensate, such as matching grants; and

(ii)   mandatory reductions in shared revenue allocations to local governments that fail to implement adequate measures to increase local-source revenue.

There are four options for devolving local government revenue raising, following the end of the TRAMPIL project, as follows:

(i)   make no changes;

(ii)   complete the job in the pilot LTAs, and hold them up as examples for other LTAs to emulate;

(iii) roll out reform to all other local governments simultaneously; or

(iv)   roll out reform to selected local governments gradually, over a predetermined period, which would require implementation in three steps:

   a.   identify the local governments to which the rollout would progressively apply;

   b.   formalize a coherent, prioritized, and appropriately sequenced improvement plan in each LTA participating in the rollout that addresses its financial and resourcing requirements for implementing reform; and

   c.   adopt and oversee a rollout timetable for each local government.

The DGFB should increase its capacity to develop policy on local tax administration and actively guide local governments along the path to reform. This involves monitoring local government reform performance and administering incentives and penalties for local governments in response to their achievement (or lack of achievement) of performance targets for local-source revenue and service delivery.

Actors outside local governments are affected by the full capture of potential local revenue. Propelling local government tax reform sustainably requires both (i) upgrading tax administration capacity that can be improved without affecting government functions beyond the local governments themselves, and (ii) engaging with the external parties that are affected by the reform.

A four-tier approach is proposed for the future reform pathway. It simultaneously tackles both internal and external demands on tax policy formulation and tax administration, as follows:

(i) At the LTA operational level, TRAMPIL must continue capacity development for the activities undertaken in the pilot local governments;

(ii) At the next level, further capacity building for local tax policy-making will be necessary for DGFB staff, as will a broader involvement by the DGFB in directing and supervising the rollout of the reform program, acting as a catalyst for the dissemination of knowledge products to local governments and facilitating change management;

(iii) A whole-of-government approach must be adopted to coordinate between the local governments and the relevant directorates at the MOF, and to coordinate the activities of the directorates themselves, particularly in the areas of joint audits, exchange of information, and the development of legislation founded on sound policy; and

(iv) A final requirement is a holistic, pan-ministry approach to strategy development. Such an approach will ensure that local tax reforms that affect areas of government outside of local government taxation are properly addressed, and that they are compatible with, or accommodated by, the policies and practices of those other areas of governance. Participants in this tier are collectively a top–down force pressuring the lower tiers to implement reform in line with the central government's wider objectives.

Further capacity building is warranted at each of the four tiers. The need for technical support is most obvious in the fields of

(i) local tax policy development;

(ii) change management;

(iii) fiscal cadastre updating;

(iv) integration of IT systems;

(v) property valuation methodology;

(vi) evaluation of the establishment of special offices for dealing with large taxpayers; and

(vii) skills development, especially in tax auditing methodology and practice (including joint audits), tax arrears collection, cost–benefit analysis, and the determination of user charges.

CHAPTER 1

INTRODUCTION

Background

Indonesia is a country of immense regional diversity in five major dimensions: geography, culture, natural resource endowments, level of economic prosperity, and standard of living.

Geographically, Indonesia comprises a land mass of just over 1.9 million square kilometers made up of 17,506 islands, more than 6,000 of which are inhabited. This great geographic expanse produces the next two discrepancies: in culture and natural resource endowments. A multitude of ethnicities and languages developed in different parts of the archipelago, and Indonesia's physiography ensured that natural resources were not bestowed equally across all parts of the country. For example, the provinces of Aceh, Riau, Central and East Java, and East Kalimantan are well-endowed with oil reserves, and Bali with natural beauty, while other regions are less favored. This diversity has obvious implications for regional economies and, therefore, in standards of living across Indonesia's regions. Regional prosperity is affected as well by human capital and its effects on the financial well-being of citizens.

The extent of economic diversity across Indonesia is evidenced by significant differences in regional gross domestic product (GDP) per capita. Figure 1 illustrates the magnitude of divergence. It shows that, in 2018, per capita GDP in the richest province, the Special Capital Region (DKI) of Jakarta, was 13.5 times higher than that in the poorest province, East Nusa Tenggara.

Figure 1: Provincial Gross Domestic Product Per Capita, 2018
(Rp '000)

Kalimantan Barat	38,794
Kalimantan Timur	174,882
Sulawesi Barat	32,124
Gorontalo	31,832
Kepulauan Riau	116,581
Kalimantan Utara	120,126
Sulawesi Tengah	50,038
Sulawesi Utara	48,118
Aceh	29,522
Riau	110,827
Kepulauan Bangka Belitung	50,052
Kalimantan Tengah	52,154
Maluku Utara	29,610
Sumatera Utara	51,417
Maluku	24,278
Sumatera Barat	42,833
Jambi	58,365
Bengkulu	33,827
Kalimantan Selatan	41,106
Sumatera Selatan	50,144
Sulawesi Tenggara	44,502
Lampung	39,864
Banten	48,457
Sulawesi Selatan	52,707
DKI Jakarta	248,306
Jawa Barat	40,306
Bali	54,618
Papua Barat	84,958
Jawa Tengah	36,784
Nusa Tenggara Timur	18,477
Papua	63,404
Jawa Timur	55,436
Special Region DI Yogyakarta	34,152
Nusa Tenggara Barat	24,707

DI = Special Region, DKI = Special Capital Region.
Note: Special regions are considered to be on the same administrative level as provincial governments.
Source: Statistics Indonesia. https://www.bps.go.id/linkTableDinamis/view/id/958.

These regional inequalities give rise to different needs for public goods and services in the various regions and, therefore, to different government expenditure requirements. Similarly, regional variation produces different levels of capacity among the local governments to raise local-source revenue and undertake local tax administration.[1]

National Economy

Indonesia is an emerging market economy, having become Southeast Asia's only trillion-dollar economy in 2017, in the wake of recent economic reform and infrastructure development. From 2011 to 2015, Indonesia's rate of economic growth declined, but it has increased each year since 2015, albeit near the average growth rate in Southeast Asia during 2015–2018 (Figure 2). In 2018, Indonesia's real GDP growth rate increased to 5.2% from 5.1% in 2017, then slowed to 5.1% in 2019 with weaker investment growth, and was expected to rise again to 5.2% in 2020 before the coronavirus disease (COVID-19) pandemic hit.[2]

Figure 2: Economic Growth Rates in Southeast Asia, 2009–2018

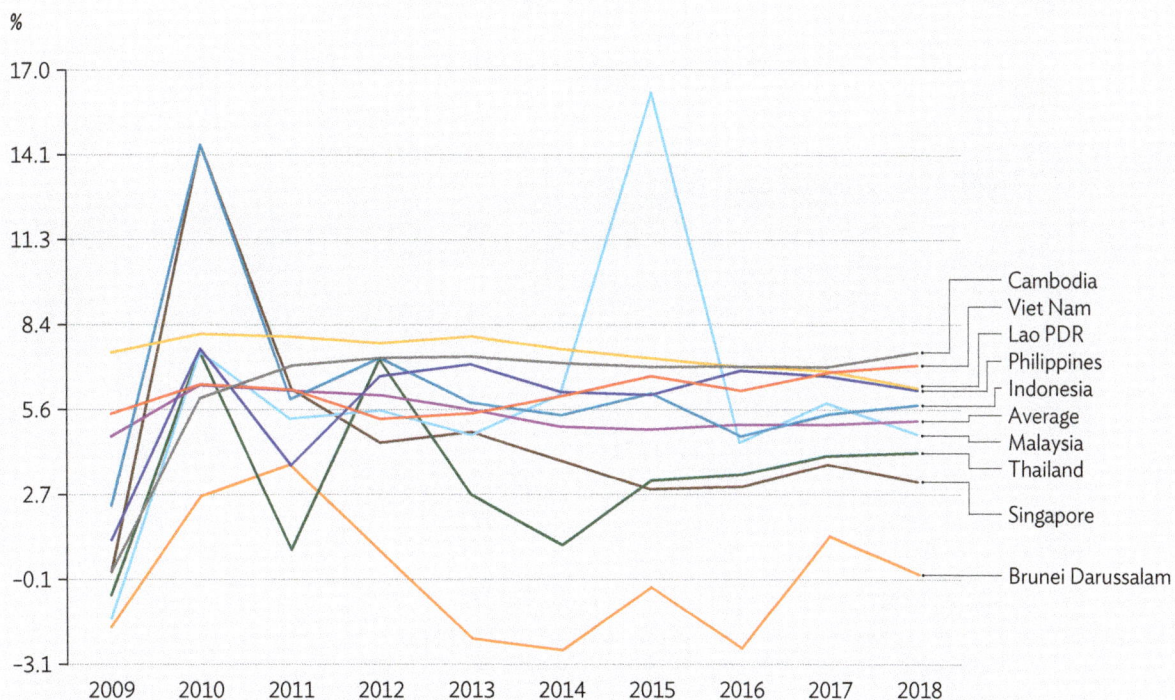

Lao PDR = Lao People's Democratic Republic.

Sources: ADB. 2019. *Key Indicators for Asia and the Pacific 2019.* Manila. https://www.adb.org/sites/default/files/publication/521981/ki2019.pdf; International Monetary Fund (IMF). IMF DataMapper. https://www.imf.org/external/datamapper/NGDP_RPCH@WEO/OEMDC/ADVEC/WEOWORLD.

---

[1]   Unless otherwise stated, "local government" is used throughout this document to mean all forms of subnational government.

[2]   World Bank. 2019. Oceans of Opportunity. *Indonesia Economic Quarterly.* June. pp. 1–2. https://openknowledge.worldbank.org/bitstream/handle/10986/31993/Indonesia-Economic-Quarterly-Oceans-of-Opportunity.pdf?sequence=7&isAllowed=y.

Despite the country's economic growth in 2018, about 26 million people, or 9.8% of the total population, were living below the government-determined national poverty line of a monthly per capita income of Rp354,386 (approximately $25). A further 55 million people, or 20.8% of the population, lived only marginally above the national poverty line.[3] This leaves nearly one-third of the population outside the country's tax base. Rectifying this situation will require an improved standard of living in Indonesia, which, as in most countries, will depend on further sustainable economic growth.

The government's fiscal balance, as of 2018, was sound. Figure 3 shows that, during 2013–2017, Indonesia imposed fiscal constraints more successfully than most of its Southeast Asian neighbors, keeping its budget deficits within a relatively narrow range equal to 2.1%–2.6% of nominal GDP. The deficit further improved to 1.8% of GDP in 2018, but widened to 2.0%–2.2% in 2019.[4]

Figure 3: Fiscal Balance as a Percentage of Nominal Gross Domestic Product in Southeast Asia, 2013–2017
(%)

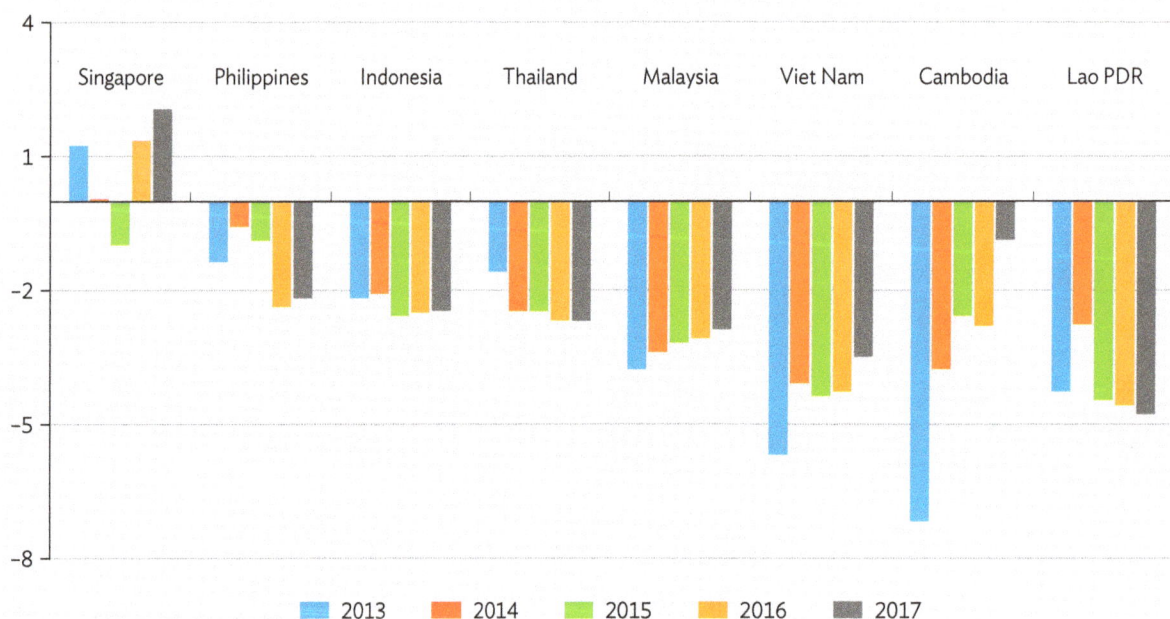

Lao PDR = Lao People's Democratic Republic.

Source: ADB. Central Government Fiscal Balance in Asia and the Pacific. https://public.tableau.com/profile/asiandevelopmentbank#!/vizhome CentralGovernmentFiscalBalanceinAsiaandthePacific/Story1.

---

3   World Bank. 2019. The World Bank in Indonesia: Overview. https://www.worldbank.org/en/country/indonesia/overview.

4   T. Diela and G. Suroyo. 2019. Indonesia 2019 Budget Deficit to Widen to Up to 2.2% amid Pressure on Revenue. *Reuters*. 25 October. https://www.nasdaq.com/articles/indonesia-2019-budget-deficit-to-widen-to-up-to-2.2-amid-pressure-on-revenue-2019-10-25.

However, with respect to the efficiency of tax collection, Indonesia fares comparatively poorly. In 2018, the ratio of taxes to GDP was 11.5%, up from 11.2% in 2017, the first increase in 5 years. That was attributable to a 6.2% increase in revenue collection over 2017, thanks primarily to higher commodity prices.[5] Nevertheless, by international standards, Indonesia's ratio of tax revenue to GDP remains very low, ranking near the bottom in Southeast Asia (Figure 4).

Figure 4: **Ratio of Tax Revenue to Gross Domestic Product in Southeast Asia, 2008–2018**
(%)

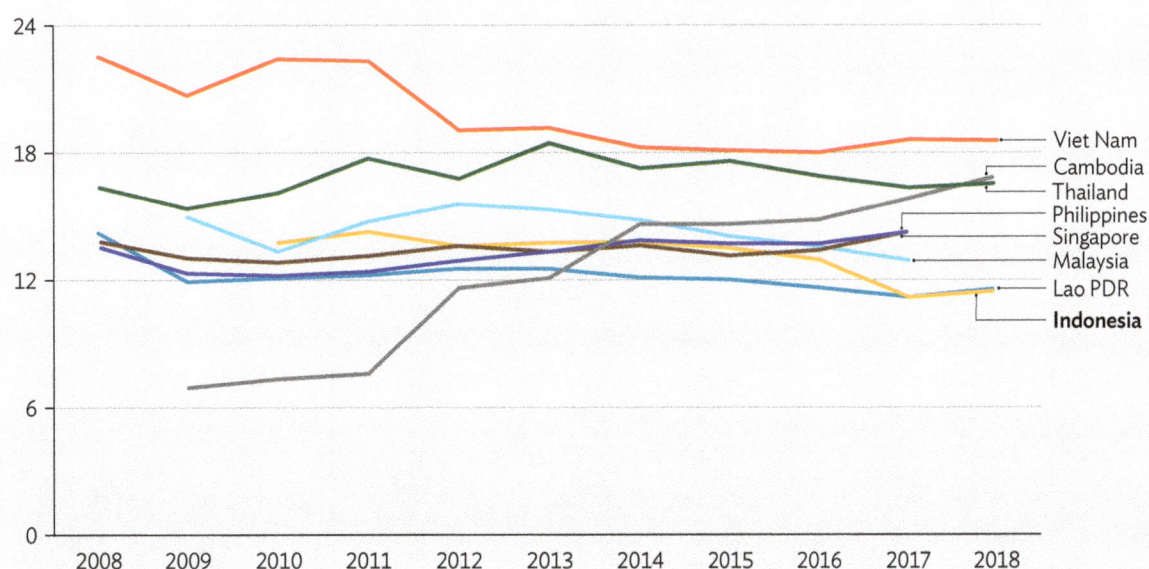

Lao PDR = Lao People's Democratic Republic.

Source: ADB. 2019. *Key Indicators for Asia and the Pacific 2019*. Manila. https://www.adb.org/sites/default/files/publication/521981/ki2019.pdf.

The key to Indonesia realizing its economic potential and thereby raising the standard of living of its citizens is economic growth, facilitated by increased domestic and foreign investment, together with human capital development. Since 2015, the Government of Indonesia has, therefore, issued a series of economic stimulus packages that have aimed to boost industrial competitiveness through deregulation and reduced red tape and to encourage exports by offering various tax incentives, notably for investment in special economic zones. The 16th economic package, released in November 2018, made increased investment the primary national economic policy objective.

---

[5]   CEIC Data Company. Indonesia Tax Revenue. https://www.ceicdata.com/en/indicator/indonesia/tax-revenue.

These national economic strategies have significant implications for local governments. Not only do their economic benefits flow directly to local regions, because that is where the central government's policies increase economic activity, but for those policies to succeed, the behavior of local governments must be consistent with them. In other words, the central government's emphasis on economic growth engendered by domestic and foreign investment should not be undercut by local government measures that run counter to that policy. In particular, local governments are subjected to limits, set either on their own initiative or by national legislation, on the extent and amount of taxation, and permissible compliance costs that they can impose on local businesses and investors to ensure coherence between their local revenue raising and the national government's broader economic goals for the country as a whole. Nevertheless, in practice, tax administration hurdles at the local level do create obstacles to the implementation of the central government's economic strategy, creating tension between investment needs and local government taxation of commerce.

Local Government Participation

Government efforts to increase regional economic prosperity vary in different countries from high central government involvement and control to extensive devolution of powers to local governments. Typical international practice supports the conventional wisdom that harnessing the full potential of sustainable economic development requires the active participation of local governments as agents of the communities that stand to benefit from such development.

The involvement of local governments necessitates the devolution to them of various powers held by the central government to enable them to provide public goods and services directly to the citizens and entities within their jurisdictions. This requires local governments to have the means to fund the expenditures thus incurred.

In recent years, local governance in Indonesia has been empowered, to a greater or lesser extent, by decentralization policies adopted by successive national governments. Developing local government taxation capacity is part of Indonesia's current political and economic reform agenda. The extent to which Indonesia has decentralized and devolved its powers of taxation is briefly reviewed in Chapter 2.

CHAPTER 2

LOCAL GOVERNANCE IN INDONESIA

Structure of Local Government

The structure of local government in Indonesia has two levels: (i) *provinsi* (provinces) and (ii) *kabupaten* (districts) and *kota* (cities).[6] Districts and cities are further subdivided into *kecamatan* (subdistricts), comprising *kelurahan* (urban wards) and/or *desa* (villages).[7] However, only provinces, districts, and cities have local governments.[8] As subdistricts and their component wards and villages are parts of districts or cities, they are not autonomous, self-governing entities. Figure 5 illustrates the hierarchical structure and the number of entities in each category.[9] Given the high population of Indonesia,[10] it is easy to understand the large numbers of entities in each category and the imperative for the central government to have a robust regulatory structure to ensure broadly congruent subnational governance.

Figure 5: Hierarchical Structure of Government in Indonesia

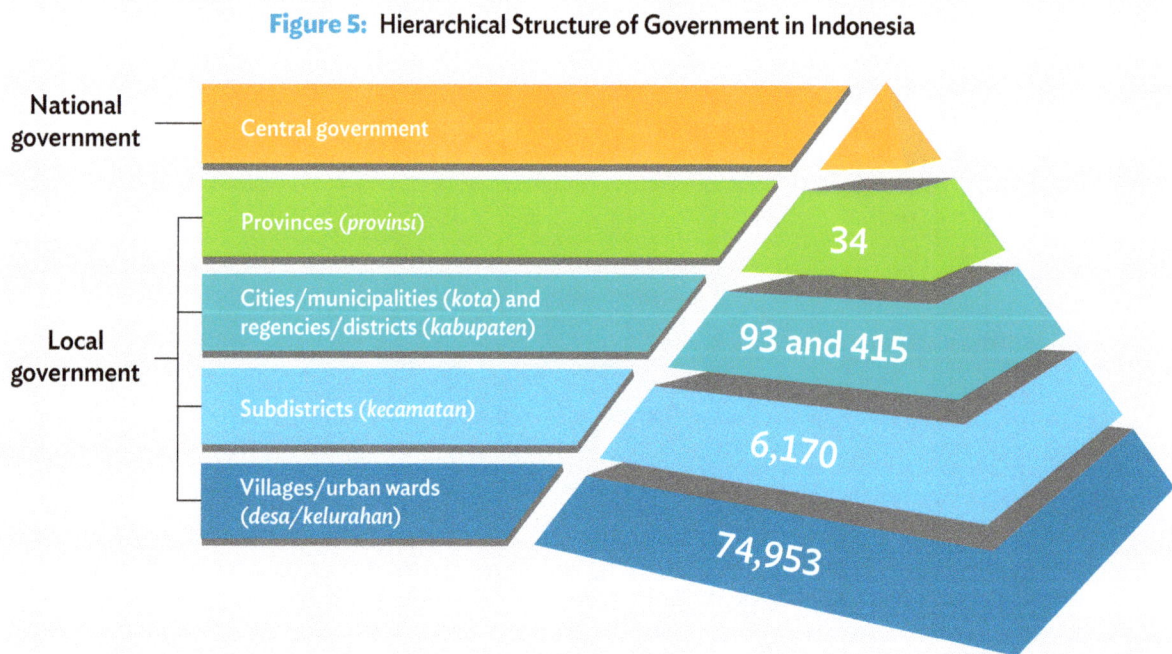

Source: Government of Indonesia, Directorate General of Fiscal Balance. Data was collected and summarized from various links from the DGFB website.

---

[6]   Article 2(1) of Law No. 23/2014 on regional administration. *Kabupaten* are also referred to as "regencies" and *kota* are also referred to as "municipalities."

[7]   Article 2(2) of Law No. 23/2014.

[8]   Article 3(1) of Law No. 23/2014.

[9]   This occurred on 31 August 2019.

[10]   The population was estimated at 270,626,000 in 2019 (United Nations. 2019. Population Division: World Population Prospects 2019. https://population.un.org/wpp/).

Decentralization and the Role of Local Governments

In general, "decentralization" can be defined as "the transfer of authority and responsibility for public functions from central government to subordinate or quasi-independent government organizations or the private sector."[11] More specifically, "fiscal decentralization" in a unitary state is the transfer of fiscal authority from the central state authority to autonomous regions. Fiscal authority includes the power to manage income (including taxation), formulate the budget, and allocate the resources owned by the region to finance the public services that the region is tasked with providing. In other words

> Fiscal decentralization is the division of public expenditure and revenue between levels of government, and the discretion given to regional and local government to determine their budgets by levying taxes and fees and allocating resources.[12]

Thus, a central government delegates its power to lower government entities—for this project's purposes, these are provinces, districts, and cities. It is this concept of decentralization that has been embraced to varying degrees by Indonesian governments, at least since the country's independence.

Local governments exist to serve the communities to which they belong by providing local services and governance, as determined by the needs and wishes of the people and entities that make up the local community. Thus, the objective of decentralization is ultimately to improve the quality and delivery of local public services.[13]

The rationale underlying decentralization policies is that the needs and preferences of individual communities are best determined locally, by community members, not by bureaucrats in the central government who are physically remote and less engaged in local affairs. This approach is intended to make it easier for the public to monitor and control the use of funds sourced from them. Thus, the central government reduces its role in addressing local needs by dispersing its authority among various subnational tiers of government that are more attuned to local requirements. In short, the intention is to decentralize certain government functions to improve the identification of local needs and responsiveness to them, thus, making the delivery of public services more effective and efficient by placing decision-making closer to the citizens who are to benefit from them.

The most obvious and direct way to make local officials more accountable and local government expenditure more efficient is to increase the share of total revenue that must be raised directly from local residents.

---

[11] J. Litvack and J. Seddon, eds. 1999. *Decentralization Briefing Notes.* Washington, DC: World Bank Institute. p. 2. http://www1.worldbank.org/publicsector/LearningProgram/Decentralization/BriefingNotes.pdf.

[12] K. Davey. 2003. *Fiscal Decentralization.* p. 8. http://unpan1.un.org/intradoc/groups/public/documents/UNTC/UNPAN017650.pdf.

[13] Decentralization also empowers local economies by giving local governments the authority to build their region's economic potential by creating healthy competition between regions and encouraging innovation.

The theory runs as follows: When local governments have to raise a significant part of their revenues using local-source taxes and charges imposed on residents, rather than receiving the same amount of funds from the central government, they become more accountable to their constituencies, and this encourages more efficient public spending and greater fiscal responsibility on the part of local governments. Put another way, shifting away from dependence on transfers from the central government by increasing revenue-generating autonomy induces greater spending efficiency because local governments are far more careful about how they spend funds when they must collect them from their own residents.

There are two further important benefits of greater revenue autonomy, as follows:

(i)   Increasing a local government's total revenue collection improves its borrowing capacity.[14] To achieve this objective, it is necessary that local governments have significant (but not unfettered) discretion in how they can raise their own revenues.

(ii)   Increasing local-source tax revenue derived by local governments reduces their dependence on fiscal transfers from the central government, which takes pressure off the central government's budget.

Aside from purely economic considerations, decentralization may also be driven by political imperatives. Indonesian history shows that greater regional autonomy has been motivated in large part by a desire to maintain cohesion in the unitary state, making decentralization a tool to counter the disintegration of the state by "diffusing social and political tensions and ensuring local cultural and political autonomy."[15] This is particularly apposite to Indonesia, an archipelagic nation with diverse social, cultural, and religious communities. The principles underlying this political objective are enshrined in the Constitution.[16]

The central government's decentralization policies shape the role of local governments. To ensure national coherence and the achievement of national objectives, and to minimize economic disparities among regions, the decentralization of governance, expenditure, and taxation powers must be formulated within a national policy framework applicable to all local governments. National policy, including standard setting and monitoring, falls under the jurisdiction of the central government, as national legislation transforms national policy into law, setting the parameters within which local governments may impose taxes on their local communities. Within this framework, functional and operational matters fall under the jurisdiction of the relevant tiers of local governments.

Thus, a sound regulatory structure sets the government's decentralization policy in a concrete, overarching form that is designed to achieve local government accountability, efficiency, and transparency. This conceptualization of the relationship between the central government and local governments is broadly reflected in current legislation concerning local governments. It is intended to be refined through proposed amendments to that legislation before the national House of Representatives.

---

[14]   In fact, the higher a region's revenue, including central government transfers, the more it may borrow. Borrowing is an appropriate way for local governments to apportion the cost of capital investments among the generations that will benefit from them.

[15]   P. Bardhan. 2002. Decentralization of Governance and Development. *Journal of Economic Perspectives.* 16(4). p. 185. https://pubs.aeaweb.org/doi/pdfplus/10.1257/089533002320951037.

[16]   See the section on "Legislation Governing Local Governments."

Evolution of Regional Autonomy in Indonesia

Regional autonomy in Indonesia has a long but checkered history. Under Dutch colonial rule, municipalities were first created in 1905, districts in 1910, and provinces on Java in the 1920s.[17] Central control remained with the Dutch administration.

At the end of the post-independence democratic period, from the end of Dutch rule in December 1949 until 1957, Law No. 1/1957 on the principles of regional government was passed with the intention of vitalizing regional autonomy. However, this effort was discontinued after the outbreak of regional rebellions in Sumatra, Sulawesi, and in West Java.

Centralization and autocracy intensified under the New Order regime from 1967 to 1997, leaving little room for meaningful decentralization. The centralist-oriented Law No. 5/1974 on governance in the regions, which set out the relationship between the central and regional governments, was enacted, but its implementing regulations were not passed until 1992, and the law itself was never fully implemented because

> the regions had to prove they were ready for implementation—and the center was the judge and the jury. An experimental implementation in 26 districts took off in 1996, which was fraught with difficulties—not least because resources and facilities were not handed over together with the tasks (footnote 17).

The two barriers to decentralization during this period were regional unrest and a lack of political will.

Two significant events triggered real decentralization reform in 1998, also called the "big bang decentralization":[18]

(i)   the Asian financial crisis during 1997–1998, which stirred up political and administrative upheaval; and

(ii) the fall of the New Order regime in 1998, which facilitated greater democratization, including pressure for greater devolution of political power from the central government to local tiers of government.[19]

Together, these two events paved the way for a series of new laws on regional autonomy and the financing of local governments. First, "[w]ithout much preparation"[20] Law No. 22/1999 on regional government and Law No. 25/1999 on revenue sharing between central and regional governments were passed at the

---

[17]   B. Hofman and K. Kaiser. 2002. Can Decentralization Help Rebuild Indonesia? *International Studies Program Working Paper Series.* No. 02-25. Atlanta: Andrew Young School of Policy Studies, Georgia State University. p. 3. https://www.issuelab.org/resources/5250/5250.pdf.

[18]   This describes "the swiftness and boldness of reforms." T. Engelmann, et al. 2015. The Devolution of the Land and Building Tax in Indonesia. *Studies.* No. 89. Bonn: German Development Institute. p. 14. https://www.econstor.eu/bitstream/10419/199214/1/die-study-89.pdf. Almost two-thirds of civil service staff, or more than 2 million employees, were transferred from the central government to various tiers of local government (footnote 17, p. 2).

[19]   Part of this change was driven by dissatisfaction with the central government's policy of exploiting natural resources without taking into account the concerns of local communities (footnote 17, p. 3).

[20]   A. Nasution. 2016. Government Decentralization Program in Indonesia. *ADBI Working Paper Series.* No. 601. Tokyo: Asian Development Bank Institute (ADBI). p. 1. https://www.adb.org/sites/default/files/publication/201116/adbi-wp601.pdf.

behest of the International Monetary Fund (IMF),[21] in which "the central government abruptly transferred political authorities and financial resources to the third level of government of Indonesia" (footnote 20).[22] Unfortunately, "the drafting of the law remained largely a bureaucratic one, with little feedback from the politicians, and even less consultations with the regions."[23] The law was criticized because "there was hardly any clarity on how much expenditure… [was] to be decentralized" while "revenue assignments were very specific" (footnote 17). For these and other political reasons—including central bureaucratic obstruction, tensions between the central and local governments and among local governments, the intrusion of vested interests of the political elite,[24] corruption, and excessive local taxes levied on businesses—both laws were amended in 2004.

Legislation Governing Local Governments

In Indonesia, the devolution of the provision of public goods to local governments has been extensive. The role of the central government is confined by law to a handful of "big ticket," nationally focused items, while local governments generally assume responsibility for matters that have a direct impact on their communities. These local government functions are divided into mandatory and optional government affairs,[25] which are undertaken by provincial and district or city governments and determined in accordance with regulated criteria.[26]

The conceptual framework for the devolution of governance powers to various tiers of local government is laid down in the Indonesian Constitution of 1945, as amended in 2000. The Constitution is, therefore, the ultimate legal basis for the devolution of powers and responsibilities to subnational governments.

Chapter VI of the Constitution deals with regional authorities and their autonomy. Article 18(1) specifies that each province, regency, and municipality shall have regional authority, which is regulated by law. Article 18(2) provides that

> [t]he regional authorities of the provinces, regencies and municipalities shall administer and manage their own affairs according to the principles of regional autonomy and the duty of assistance…

---

[21] This was a requirement in connection with an IMF bailout worth $43 billion to help Indonesia cope with the Asian financial crisis. B. Sudibyo, K. G. Kwik, and S. Sabirin. 2000. *Letter of Intent of the Government of Indonesia*. Jakarta. https://www.imf.org/external/np/loi/2000/idn/01/.

[22] The autonomous operational functions were devolved to the districts and cities and to the subdistricts beneath them. By a quirk of fate, although not originally intended, the provinces were retained under Law No. 22/1999, though they played a relatively minor role in governance of districts and cities.

[23] Footnote 17, p. 4.

[24] This is often called "elite capture."

[25] Article 6(2) of Government Regulation No. 38/2007 on the division of government affairs among the (central) government, provincial government, and regency/city governments. These functions are set out in extensive lists in Article 7 of this regulation.

[26] Article 4(1) of Government Regulation No. 38/2007.

The first steps toward putting these constitutional principles into practice were taken on 23 November 1945, when Law No. 1/1945 on the position of the regional national committee was enacted to establish regional committees to govern local areas.

Article 18(5) of the Constitution confers extremely "wide-ranging autonomy" on regional authorities. In effect, they have power over all matters except those that are specified by law to reside with the central government. The central government is concerned with ensuring the survival of the nation as a whole. Thus, Law No. 32/2004 on local governance stipulates that the areas under the control of the central government are foreign policy, defense, security, judicial policy, national monetary and fiscal policy, and religious affairs.[27]

Additionally, Article 1(4) of Government Regulation No. 38/2007 on the division of government affairs among the (central) government, provincial government, and regency/city governments defines "regional autonomy" as

> the right, authority, and obligation of [an] autonomous region to regulate and manage government affairs and the interests of the local community in accordance with the laws and regulations.

To exercise that "wide-ranging autonomy," Article 18(6) empowers regional authorities to pass their own regulations: "The regional authorities shall have the authority to adopt regional regulations and other regulations to implement autonomy and the duty of assistance." Again, Government Regulation 38/2007 elucidates:

> Government regulations are functions of government that are the rights and obligations of each level and/or structure of government to regulate and manage these functions that are their authority in order to protect, serve, empower and prosper the community.

However, Article 18(7) ensures that the structure and administrative mechanisms that regulate local governments are, in effect, controlled by the central government: "The structure and administrative mechanisms of regional authorities shall be regulated by law"—or the laws passed by the national House of Representatives.

On 18 August 2000, Chapter VI of the Constitution was amended with the addition of Article 18A, to regulate the relationship between the central government and local governments, and Article 18B, to recognize the uniqueness of certain regional authorities and to recognize traditional communities and their customary rights. These amendments entrenched the manner of regional governance in Indonesia. Article 18A is of primary concern here.

---

[27] Article 10(3) of Law 32/2004. However, read in conjunction with Article 18(5) of the Constitution, the meaning of Article 10(5) of Law 32/2004, which prescribes how the central government may carry out administrative affairs that "become the authority of the Government other than those as meant in paragraph (3)," is quite unclear.

Article 18A(1) specifies that national law governs the relationships between the central government and local governments, and between local governments. Those laws must recognize the particularities and diversity of each region.[28]

Of particular significance to this publication is Article 18A(2) of the Constitution, which governs financial relations between the central government and local governments. Article 18A(2) states:

> The relations between the central government and regional authorities in finances, public services, and the use of natural and other resources shall be regulated and administered with justice and equity according to law.

Therefore, national law again determines the financing powers and entitlements of local governments. Because of the central government's obligation under Law 32/2004 to control monetary and fiscal policy, a local government's ability to raise its own revenue must fall within criteria set by the central government. This must be the overriding imperative to resolve the inherent conflict between the financial autonomy of local governments and prudent national fiscal policy—and, to a lesser extent, between local government borrowing and national monetary policy—in the interest of sustaining a coherent unitary state.

In line with constitutional requirements, a series of detailed national legislation was passed concerning regional administration, the fiscal relationship between the central government and local governments, and local taxes and charges, as follows:

(i)   Law No. 1 of 1945 on the position of the regional national committee,

(ii)   Law No. 1 of 1957 on local governments,

(iii)   Law No. 5 of 1974 on regional local governments,

(iv)   Law No. 18 of 1997 on regional taxes and charges,

(v)   Law No. 22 of 1999 on regional government,

(vi)   Law No. 25 of 1999 on revenue sharing between central and regional governments,

(vii)   Law No. 34 of 2000 on the amendment to Law 18/1997,

(viii) Law No. 32 of 2004 on local governance,

(ix)   Law No. 33 of 2004 on fiscal balance between central and regional governments,

(x)   Law No. 36 of 2008 on the fourth amendment to Law No. 7 of 1983 on income tax,

(xi)   Law No. 25 of 2009 on public service,

(xii)   Law No. 28 of 2009 on regional taxes and charges, and

(xiii) Law No. 23 of 2014 on local government.

---

[28]   The principal relevant national laws are currently Law No. 33/2004 on fiscal balance between the central government and the regional governments, and Law No. 28/2009 on local taxes and charges.

Appendix 1 presents this legislative progression, the principal effects of the original laws, and the replacement of earlier deficient laws by later ones. Ultimately, the amendments to the Constitution, together with the 21st century laws, "firmly embedded regional autonomy in Indonesia's system of government."[29]

Sources of Local Government Revenue

International experience shows that the formula for creating an effective local public sector is responsive and responsible local government. Local governments must have the fiscal capacity to provide the desired regional services and infrastructure. The extent to which local governments can best achieve their objectives depends to a large degree on their ability to generate their own revenue.

In Indonesia, local government public service improvement is constrained by a lack of adequate self-financing in cities, and particularly in districts, which depend heavily on transfers from the central government. This is because of (i) the limited powers conferred on local governments to impose taxes, (ii) the lack of resources and administrative capacity of local governments to effectively assess and collect taxes when they have the power to do so, and (iii) limited local government power to borrow.

The success of regional autonomy in Indonesia depends, to a large extent, on local governments deriving sufficient revenue to cover their expenditures needed to supply the goods and services they are mandated by law to provide. The principle of fiscal decentralization means that assigning responsibility for expenditure to local governments must be accompanied by granting them the authority to tax. This was effectuated by the passage of Law 22/1999, Law 25/1999, and Law 34/2000. Until then, local government expenditure was funded principally through transfers of earmarked grants from the central government. Law 22/1999 transferred specific taxing powers from the central government to district and city governments. Simultaneously, Law 25/1999 increased the local governments' share of central government revenue from natural resources, and Law 34/2000 granted more general taxing powers to local governments.

Historically, Indonesia has adopted fiscal decentralization for expenditure, not revenue, which has meant that the central government prioritized transfers to local governments to improve their capacity to manage spending. Meanwhile, considerable scope remains for local governments to augment their local-source revenue. Urban local governments, in particular, have the potential to increase revenues because of their large economies and populations.

This last point is borne out by regional revenue statistics compiled by the Directorate General of Fiscal Balance (DGFB). Across all subnational governments, the ratio of local government tax to GDP stood at 1.1% in 2012. By 2018, it had reached only 1.3%.[30] Figure 6 shows that the increase in the ratio of own-source revenue to local government expenditure was similarly slight over the 7-year period, rising from 38.9% in 2012 to only 40.7% in 2018. In the districts, that ratio reached only 32.2% in 2018. These statistics demonstrate that the efforts to move toward higher autonomous funding have generally been ineffective, at least up to 2018.

---

[29]   Footnote 17, p. 6.

[30]   The 2018 statistics cited here are those recorded by the DGFB on 17 December 2019.

Figure 6: **Proportion of Local-Source Revenue to Local Government Expenditure, 2012 and 2018**

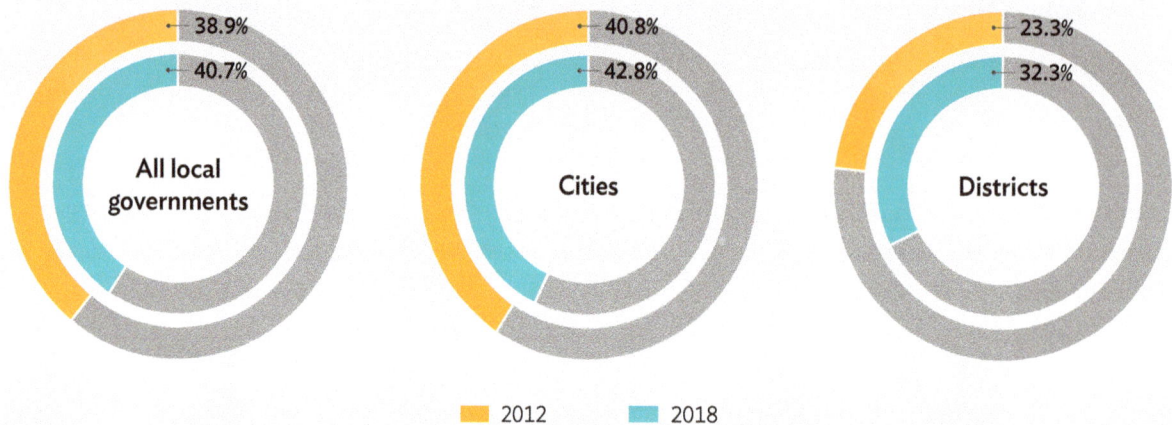

Source: Government of Indonesia, Directorate General of Fiscal Balance (DGFB). *Realisasi Anggaran Pendapatan dan Belanja Daerah (Realization of the Regional Revenue and Expenditure Budget).* Jakarta (2 years: 2012 and 2018).

Funding sources for local government expenditure fall into three broad categories, as follows:

(i)   locally generated revenue (PAD), comprising

   a.   locally imposed taxes,

   b.   charges for services supplied within a local government's jurisdiction,

   c.   profits from locally owned state-owned enterprises, and

   d.   other locally sourced revenue such as interest on investments;

(ii)   central government transfers, in the form of distributions from

   a.   revenue sharing fund (DBH),

   b.   the general allocation fund (DAU), and

   c.   the special allocation fund (DAK); and

(iii) borrowing.

PAD consists primarily of local government tax revenue. Article 2 of Law 28/2009 stipulates 16 types of local taxes, 11 of which are district or city taxes, and the other five are provincial taxes. In addition, there are 31 types of levies for which the law gives local governments the authority to determine the rates.[31]

The range of local government taxes currently imposed under Article 2 of Law 28/2009 is summarized in Appendix 2, which divides taxes into provincial and district or city, and then subdivides them between those levied based on official assessment or self-assessment.

---

[31]   See Articles 110, 127, and 141 of Law 28/2009.

Figure 7: Allocation of Provincial Taxes to Districts and Cities

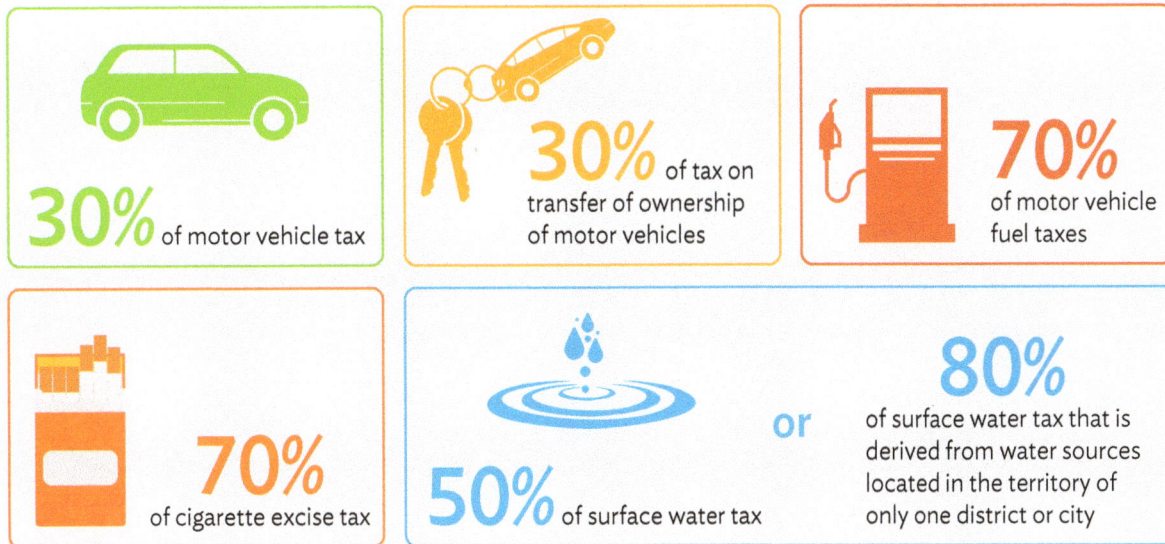

30% of motor vehicle tax

30% of tax on transfer of ownership of motor vehicles

70% of motor vehicle fuel taxes

70% of cigarette excise tax

50% of surface water tax

or

80% of surface water tax that is derived from water sources located in the territory of only one district or city

Source: Asian Development Bank, Tax Revenue Administration Modernization and Policy Improvement in Local Governments project.

Law 28/2009 requires that portions of the proceeds of provincial tax revenue be allocated to districts and cities in the province. Article 94 sets out the shares to be allocated to the districts and cities (Figure 7).

The DBH has a direct relationship to the tax-generating ability of a particular region. It represents tax revenues collected by the central government under the national taxation apparatus, or by provincial governments, from taxpayers in the various regions. These tax revenues are then allocated back to subordinate regions by a formula broadly based on their contributions, such that they are shared in relation to their origin. For example, with the land and building tax for mining, forestry, and plantations (PBB-P3), some regions such as East Kalimantan, Aceh, Riau, and Papua receive very high amounts from the DBH because they have significant endowments of natural resources on which the PBB-P3 is levied. Similarly, under Article 31C of Law 7/1983, as amended by Law 36/2008, 20% of personal income taxes collected by the central government are allocated to the district and city governments on the basis of taxpayer residence. Such allocations from the DBH give no incentive for local governments to seek additional PAD.

The diversity of economic activity and development, income level, and wealth accumulation across Indonesia's provinces, districts, and cities sharply affects the ability of different local governments to impose local taxes and user charges, and to generate their own and shared revenues from their jurisdiction. This constraint is exacerbated by limited administrative capacity in many of those local governments.[32]

---

[32]   This point is discussed further in Chapter 3.

As a result, most local governments suffer a fiscal gap, which necessitates redistribution by the central government to effect fiscal equalization. The objective of redistribution is to transfer government revenue derived from richer regions to poorer regions so that each region has more or less the same ability to provide public services as required. In Indonesia, the fiscal gap is filled mainly by DAU transfers from the central government.[33]

Formulaically, a fiscal gap is

$$\text{Fiscal needs} - \text{Fiscal capacity}$$

where *fiscal needs* are determined by the local government's total expenditure requirements,[34] and

$$\text{Fiscal capacity} = \text{PAD} + \text{DBH}$$

therefore,

$$\text{Fiscal gap} = \text{Fiscal needs} - (\text{PAD} + \text{DBH})$$

Thus, local governments that lack a robust economic base for the imposition of extensive local taxes and for producing shared revenues suffer a wider fiscal gap, and are far more dependent on DAU transfers from the central government, than those local governments that have robust economic bases. This discrepancy is illustrated in Figure 8, which shows the relatively high dependency of cities and, even more so, of districts on central government DAU transfers in 2018. By comparison, because it is an economic powerhouse, DKI Jakarta received no DAU transfers at all. Figure 8 points to a need for greater focus on locally sourced revenue, particularly in cities and districts, and for incentives to produce it.

An important negative feature of the current intergovernmental transfer system in Indonesia is its bias against urban populations because the central government initially distributes equal DAU funding to districts without regard for demographics. Increased local government revenue autonomy would, therefore, allow urban local governments to mobilize the revenue that they need.

The DAK is the source of specific grants from the state revenue and expenditure budget to certain local governments to fund special local government activities or projects that align with national priorities regarding, for example, regional health, education, and road infrastructure. It is, thus, used to close interregional gaps in infrastructure for the provision of public services.

---

[33] Broadly, the current DAU allocation from the central government is 26% of the total domestic revenue minus the shared revenue.

[34] This is measured with reference to a variety of indicators, including population, area, construction indexes, the human development index, and regional GDP.

Figure 8: Comparative Local Government Revenue Sources, 2018

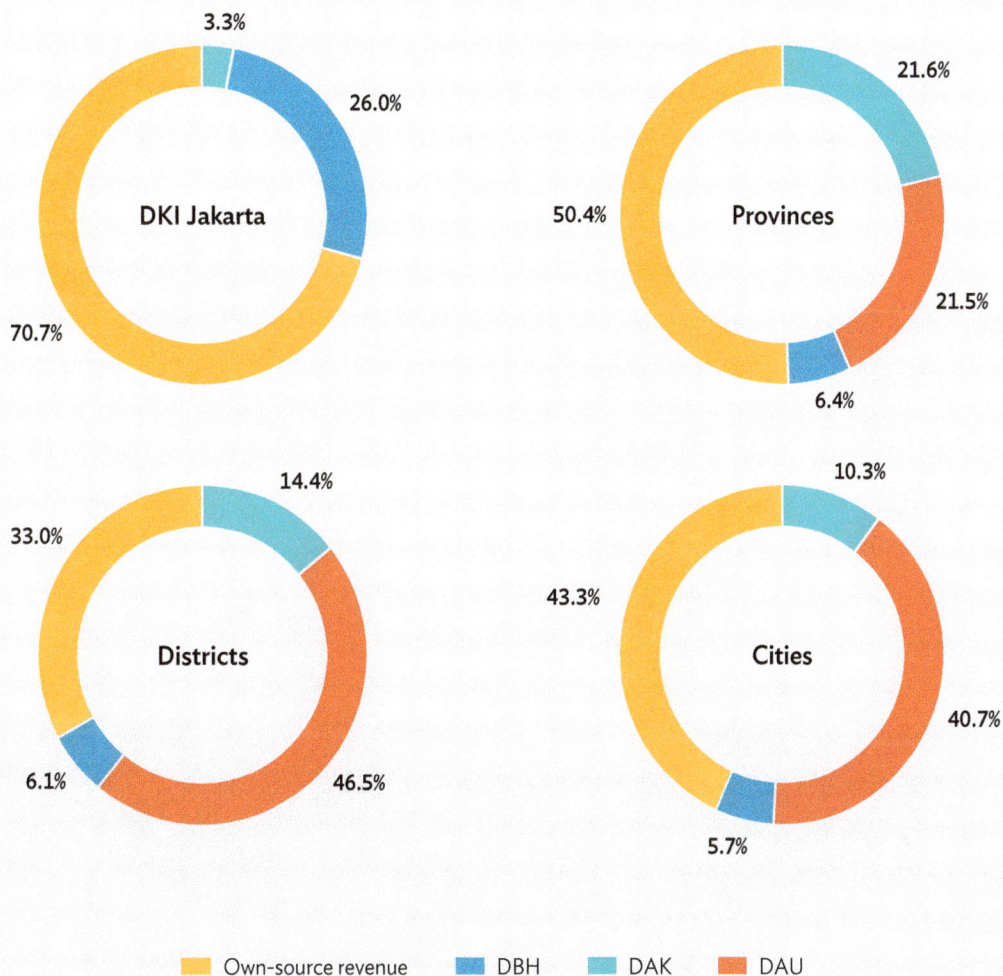

DAK = special allocation fund, DAU = general allocation fund, DBH = revenue sharing fund.

Note: The statistics used here are those recorded by the Directorate General of Fiscal Balance on 25 October 2019.

Source: Government of Indonesia, Directorate General of Fiscal Balance. *Realisasi Anggaran Pendapatan dan Belanja Daerah 2018 (Realization of the Regional Revenue and Expenditure Budget 2018)*. Jakarta.

An upshot of inadequate revenue-yielding district and city taxes is significant transfer dependency and attendant lack of accountability and fiscal responsibility in local governments, as well as inefficient expenditure. While putting pressure on the central government's fiscal balance, transfer dependency constricts the ability of local governments to adequately fund expenditure on the public services demanded by their constituents.

Several steps can be taken to augment local government capacity in tax policy formulation and tax administration. A selection of remedial measures to improve the capacity of local tax administrations is discussed in detail in Chapter 3, and further policy initiatives are addressed in Chapter 4.

CHAPTER 3

IMPROVING LOCAL GOVERNMENT TAX POLICY AND ADMINISTRATION

Policy Achievements under TRAMPIL

The technical assistance for the Tax Revenue Administration Modernization and Policy Improvement in Local Governments (TRAMPIL) project was designed to help the Directorate General of Fiscal Balance (DGFB) develop local government revenue policy and legislation, impart policy advice on local government taxation initiatives, and assist the Ministry of Finance (MOF) with legislative reform to clarify and integrate disparate national and local tax policies.

TRAMPIL also aimed to build capacity through the delivery of training via focus group discussions, as well as knowledge-sharing products for DGFB staff to use to improve their capacity to formulate policy on local taxes, and to build the capacity of local government staff.

To achieve these objectives, TRAMPIL drew on its policy development work to produce academic papers, analytical reports, and policy briefs to support amendments to Law 28/2009. Focus group discussions were held in conjunction with these outputs. The analytical work addressed the following:

(i)   local tax policy, revenue mobilization, and intergovernmental transfer policies;

(ii)   the impact of devolution of land and building tax for mining, forestry, and plantations (PBB-P3);

(iii)   alternative simplified modeling of property valuations;

(iv)   local government business and income tax surcharges;

(v)   compliance with local taxes; and

(vi)   policies on user charges.

TRAMPIL also provided policy briefs to support the drafting of an academic paper underpinning the revision of Law 28/2009, which covered

(i)   the choice between value-added versus retail sales taxes to replace local sales taxes on services,

(ii)   models for revenue sharing between provinces and their districts and cities aimed at minimizing manipulation by provincial governments,

(iii)   local government taxes piggybacking on national taxes,

(iv)   tobacco excise taxes,

(v)   taxes on motor vehicles, and

(vi)   taxes on water extraction.

Moreover, as much of local government tax administration law overlaps Law No. 6 of 1983 on general taxation provisions and procedures, TRAMPIL proposed that laws governing local government and central government tax administration be synchronized to remove inconsistencies and streamline tax administration across all taxes in Indonesia. If that recommendation is adopted, it would seem to render superfluous one of two separate laws that state essentially the same thing. It is suggested that Law 6/1983 be amended to incorporate the administration of local government taxes and charges as well.

This sort of rationalization can be extended for further efficiencies. Since all tax types are the same for all local governments within each category—whether provincial, district, or city—further scope remains to standardize procedures, such as property valuation methodology, information and communication technology (ICT) systems, fiscal cadastre formatting, statistical data-reporting formats, debt-collection methodology, and training across all local governments. Given the large number of local governments in Indonesia, such standardization offers potentially enormous economies of scale and mitigation of regional differences, which would benefit the country as a whole. This is an example of how a holistic approach could address local government revenue mobilization. If such an approach were adopted, regional autonomy would not be compromised. In accordance with their particular priorities, individual local governments would still be free to select which taxes to impose, exemptions to allow, and tax rates to apply—all within the limitations set by the amended Law 28/2009—and they would still directly collect the taxes that they elect to levy.

In summary, TRAMPIL policy recommendations advanced the following objectives: providing adequate funding for local government services by improving the collection of existing taxes and introducing new taxes, including a single, unified local business tax; greater efficiency in local taxation and an improved economic environment for local businesses and development by tightening the "closed list" of extant taxes and eliminating many license fees through the introduction of a local business tax; and better accountability and more efficient expenditure by increasing the share of local government revenue raised through local taxes levied on local residents.

From this work, it is evident that Indonesia has significant potential national and local-source tax revenue that could fund local government expenditure. To a significant extent, short- to medium-term policy and legislative measures have been addressed in the proposed amendments to Law 28/2009 and Law 33/2004 to capture that potential revenue. However, further policy initiatives can still be developed. Crucially, they would formulate details for the operation of regional incentive funds (DID), as proposed in amendments to Law 33/2004.

Notwithstanding whatever policy developments are carried out in the short to medium term, policy directions need to be devised to broaden the local government tax base over the long term by adding features to the local government regime of taxes and charges that have not been incorporated into proposed amendments to Law 28/2009.

Box 1 summarizes TRAMPIL policy contributions to the local government tax reform agenda.

Proposed Changes to Law 28/2009

The objectives of amending Law 28/2009 are to

(i)   expand the local government tax base to better enable local governments, especially of districts and cities, to fund their expenditure responsibilities by adding new types of taxes;

(ii)   enable better implementation of local government taxes and levies that are compatible with other laws and regulations; and

(iii) remove distortions and economic inefficiency that arise under the existing law.

Box 1: Key TRAMPIL Achievements in Local Government Tax Policy

The contributions of the TRAMPIL project included the following:

(i)   proposals of amendments to Law 28/2009 to provide feedback to the Directorate General of Fiscal Balance, as well as to formulate recommendations for revisions;

(ii)   academic papers, analytical reports, and policy briefs delivered to support amendments to Law 28/2009;

(iii)   policy briefs on

    a.   value-added versus retail sales tax to replace current local government taxes on services,

    b.   revenue-sharing models for provinces and their districts and cities,

    c.   piggybacking on national taxes,

    d.   tobacco excise taxes,

    e.   taxes on motor vehicles, and

    f.   taxes on water extraction; and

(iv)   focus group discussions conducted on

    a.   local tax policy,

    b.   revenue mobilization,

    c.   intergovernmental transfer policies,

    d.   the impact of devolution of PBB-P3,

    e.   simplified tax object valuation modeling,

    f.   surcharges on national taxes, and

    g.   user charges.

PBB-P3 = land and building tax for mining, forestry, and plantations; TRAMPIL = Tax Revenue Administration Modernization and Policy Improvement in Local Governments.
Source: ADB. 2020. TRAMPIL Final Report. Jakarta. Unpublished.

These objectives are to be achieved within the parameters of the central government's macroeconomic policies, particularly those that encourage investment and economic development in the regions.

Some tax objects in Law 28/2009 were removed through either judicial decisions or the application of *lex posterior derogat legi priori*, under which conflicting provisions of legislation passed after Law 28/2009 was enacted override the provisions in Law 28/2009. These include the following:

(i)   Decision 52/PUU-IX/2011 of the Constitutional Court, which revoked Article 42(2)(g) of Law 28/2009 by declaring that golf could not be included as an object of the entertainment tax;

(ii)   Decision 46/PUU-XII/2014 of the Constitutional Court, concerning the calculation of the telecommunication tower control levy;

(iii)   Article 79A of Law 23/2006, concerning *administrasi kependudukan* (population administration) as inserted by Article 19 of Law No. 24/2013 on population administration, which provides that the issuance and administration of population documents shall be free of charge, while Article 110(1)(c) of Law 28/2009 includes the printing of resident identity cards and civil registry deeds as tax objects that can be subjected to a charge for the rendering of public services; and

(iv)   Law 25/2009, which requires that the cost of certain public services prescribed by law to be the responsibility of the central government and borne by it, while Law 28/2009 authorizes local charges for roadside parking, motor vehicle testing services, and the inspection and testing of firefighting equipment.

Proposed amendments to Law 28/2009 convert the current 16 types of local government taxes into four broad categories based on their underlying characteristics: consumption taxes, property taxes, natural resource taxes, and *opsen* (surcharges) on national taxes. Within these four categories, there are six specific local government taxes, as follows:

(i)   *Consumption taxes*: motor vehicle tax and taxes on certain goods and services,

(ii) *Property taxes*: land and buildings taxes,

(iii) *Natural resource taxes*: taxes on certain natural resources, and

(iv) *Surcharges on national taxes*: surcharge on the tobacco excise tax and surcharge on the personal income tax.

This grouping of tax types is intended to simplify the local government tax regimes and facilitate the rationalization of local government regulations, especially outdated and conflicting ones,[35] thereby reducing the drafting and administration costs incurred by local tax administrations (LTAs), as well as compliance costs incurred by taxpayers. The focus of the regulations issued under the amended law will be on the imposition of a local government tax and the tax rates, which local governments have the authority to determine within maximums prescribed by the law.[36]

Further simplification of the law is effected by eliminating many license fees through the introduction of local business taxes. These measures are important because they will reduce compliance costs and the perception among some companies and entrepreneurs that Indonesia has an antibusiness climate.

The proposed amendments to Law 28/2009 were expected to substantially increase local governments' local-source revenue collections.

Notwithstanding the obvious benefits of reforming Law 28/2009, progress has been very slow, with draft amendments still pending.[37] They were not included on the list of 50 bills prioritized for debate in 2020, and it remains uncertain when they will be taken up for debate.

The proposed amendments to Law 28/2009 were coupled with proposed amendments to Law 33/2004, which regulates the sharing of central government tax revenues with local governments. This amendment was ranked 12th on the National Legislation Program, 2015–2019 list, but does not appear at all on the 2020–2024 list (footnote 37). The lack of progress in the legislature on both pieces of legislation may be circumvented to some extent by including selected reforms in the Omnibus Law. This approach is intended to streamline certain central government tax laws, and so facilitate investment and ease of doing business, thereby expanding employment. To facilitate progress toward local government tax reform, this procedure should be considered when the government is attempting to enact amendments to Law 28/2009 and Law 33/2004 that enjoy broad support.

---

[35]   The number of local government tax regulations currently exceeds 5,000, many of which repeat the law.

[36]   However, the proposed amendments allow the central government to reduce local taxes and levy rates by presidential regulation whenever the central government considers that local taxes would otherwise contravene its fiscal policy.

[37]   Indonesian Centre for Law & Policy Studies. 2019. *Program Legislasi Nasional Rancangan Undang-Undang Tahun, 2020–2024* (in Indonesian). https://pshk.or.id/wp-content/uploads/2019/12/PSHK-Prolegnas-2020-2024-.pdf.

Legislative delays in confronting structural problems in the financing of local government expenditure clearly limit the ability of local governments to innovate new ways to produce revenue from local sources, and they raise questions about the legislative commitment to reform. Fortunately, despite the procrastination, local government revenue generation can be substantially improved, as Law 28/2009 is now strengthening the capacity and processes of tax administration, as demonstrated by the TRAMPIL pilot local governments.

Success Achieved by TRAMPIL in Pilot Local Governments

TRAMPIL efforts to improve tax administration in four pilot local governments produced numerous outputs that have benefited the pilot areas and provided valuable insights into the potential benefits for other local authorities that may adopt similar measures to enhance their revenues. The more important success stories are described below.

Development of Comprehensive Fiscal Cadastre Databases

Internationally, annual property taxes are a principal means by which local governments raise local-source tax revenue. Property taxation is attractive for its stable revenue flow due to the inelastic supply of land, efficient collection, and relatively even distribution across taxpayers. It is not distortionary, and so is neutral regarding central government investment and economic growth objectives. Further, it mitigates wealth inequality because wealthier people own more property of greater value on which higher annual property taxes are levied. This point is especially relevant in Indonesia where in mid-2018, the wealthiest 1% of households were estimated to hold 46.6% of the country's total wealth, the wealthiest 5% held 65.4%, and the wealthiest 10% held 75.3%, with 84.2% of all wealth estimated to be nonfinancial assets, mostly land and buildings.[38] Property taxes are also difficult to avoid—*provided that a comprehensive fiscal cadastre is in place.*

Two types of local government property taxation are levied in Indonesia: (i) the urban and rural land and building tax (PBB-P2), and (ii) the tax on the transfer of rights to land and buildings (BPHTB) (Appendix 2). Imposed by districts, cities, and DKI Jakarta, PBB-P2 accounted for 25.9% of its local-source revenue in 2018, and BPHTB for 24.5%, adding up to 50.4%.

As shown in Table 1, PBB-P2 and BPHTB were the two dominant types of local-source taxation for three TRAMPIL pilot local governments: the cities of Balikpapan and Bandung and the province of DKI Jakarta[39]—though for Balikpapan, the single most important tax was the street lighting tax. Badung is an exception, given that it is a district in Indonesia's internationally renowned tourist island, Bali, where the hotel tax dominates.

---

[38]   Credit Suisse Research Institute. 2018. *Global Wealth Databook 2018*. Zurich. pp. 146 and 155. The high share of nonfinancial wealth reflects both the importance of land and agricultural assets and the rural residents' relative lack of access to financial services (p. 6).

[39]   Special regions are considered to be on the same level as provincial governments but for comparative purposes, the provincial taxes collected by DKI Jakarta are ignored.

Table 1: **Percentage Contributions to Directly Assessed Local-Source Tax Revenue in the Pilot Local Governments, 2018 (%)**

Tax	Badung	Balikpapan	Bandung	DKI Jakarta[a]	National Average
PBB-P2	5.3	19.0	25.6	40.9	25.9
BPHTB	12.9	18.1	27.3	21.6	24.5
Subtotal: PBB-P2 and BPHTB	**18.2**	**37.1**	**52.9**	**62.5**	**50.4**
Hotel tax	57.7	9.3	13.9	8.0	9.2
Restaurant tax	16.1	17.6	15.1	14.5	12.7
Parking service tax	0.6	4.2	2.0	2.4	1.6
Entertainment tax	2.1	5.1	4.1	3.8	2.7
Advertising tax	0.1	1.9	1.1	4.7	2.6
Street lighting tax	3.6	24.1	9.3	3.6	17.5
Groundwater tax	1.6	0.5	1.6	0.5	0.9
Nonmetallic minerals tax	0.0	0.2	0.0	0.0	2.4
Swallows' nest tax	0.0	0.0	0.0	0.0	0.0
Total	**100.0**	**100.0**	**100.0**	**100.0**	**100.0**

BPHTB = tax on transfer of rights in land and buildings, DKI = Special Capital Region, PBB-P2 = urban and rural land and building tax.

[a] This data is provisional.

Sources: Asian Development Bank, Tax Revenue Administration Modernization and Policy Improvement in Local Governments project; Government of Indonesia, Directorate General of Fiscal Balance. 2019. *Realisasi APBD, 2018.* Jakarta.

Figure 9 indicates that the contribution of property taxes to the pilot local governments' local-source tax bases was reasonably consistent over the 5 years from 2014 to 2018, except in Balikpapan, which experienced a decline from 63% in 2014 to 37% in 2018.

The importance of property taxes to local government revenue—especially in DKI Jakarta, where they supply nearly two-thirds of local-source nonprovincial tax revenue—illustrates the imperative to establish and maintain reliable fiscal cadastre databases for PBB-P2 and transfer-value data for BPHTB. The veracity of the transfer-value data for BPHTB is especially significant because it affects the tax object sales value adopted in PBB-P2 assessments. Problems arise where the registration of property transfers is delayed to defer BPHTB liability.

When PBB-P2 was transferred from the central government to local governments during 2010–2014, the Tax Object Information Management System (SISMIOP), which contained software and information technology (IT) applications to manage property tax data, was not up to date—and it largely remains out of date even though Article 79(2) of Law 28/2009 prescribes that property be assessed every 3 years.[40] Reliable property valuations should be obtainable by local governments, which are in the best position to identify and assess their local properties.

[40] Or assessments could be done annually for tax object values that can be assessed each year.

Figure 9: Contribution of Property Taxes to Local-Source Tax Revenue in the Pilot Local Governments, 2014–2018 (%)

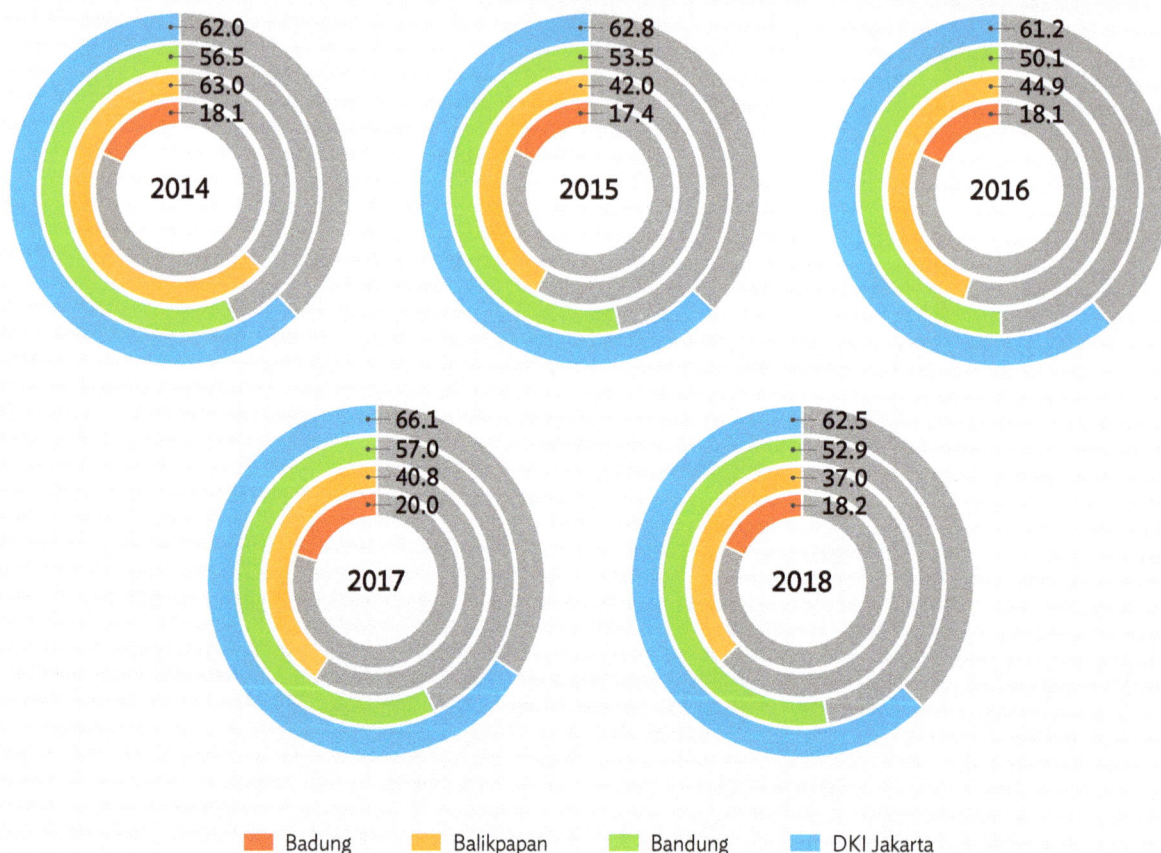

DKI = Special Capital Region.

Sources: Asian Development Bank, Tax Revenue Administration and Policy Improvement in Local Governments project; Government of Indonesia, Directorate General of Fiscal Balance. 2018. *Realisasi Anggaran Pendapatan dan Belanja Daerah 2018 (Realization of the Regional Revenue and Expenditure Budget 2018)*. Jakarta: Statistics Indonesia.

Given the importance of PBB-P2 to local government tax revenue and the shortcomings of SISMIOP data, upgrading pilot local governments' fiscal cadastres became a dominant part of the TRAMPIL project. The main improvement in their fiscal cadastre databases was to incorporate more comprehensive and accurate coverage of properties and their owners, and to produce fair and reasonably reliable valuations. Table 2 compares that process with existing practices by local governments. Continued external support to local governments will generally be required to make fiscal cadastres adequately comprehensive. Figure 10 illustrates the methodology behind the TRAMPIL approach.

Table 2: Comparison between Local Government Practice and TRAMPIL Methodology

Existing Local Government Practice	TRAMPIL Methodology
Limited use of information technology	Extensive use of information technology
(i) Use of paper forms	(i) Use of mobile applications
(ii) Lack of a systematic survey plan	(ii) Systematic survey plan using drones
(iii) Text data only	(iii) Text and image data
(iv) Manual data entry	(iv) Direct data transfer to server
Time Lag in Monitoring Survey Results	**Real-Time Monitoring of Survey Results**
Survey focus on a single tax object	Integrated survey covering many tax objects

TRAMPIL = Tax Revenue Administration Modernization and Policy Improvement in Local Governments.
Source: Asian Development Bank, TRAMPIL project.

Figure 10: TRAMPIL Methodology of Fiscal Cadastre Updating

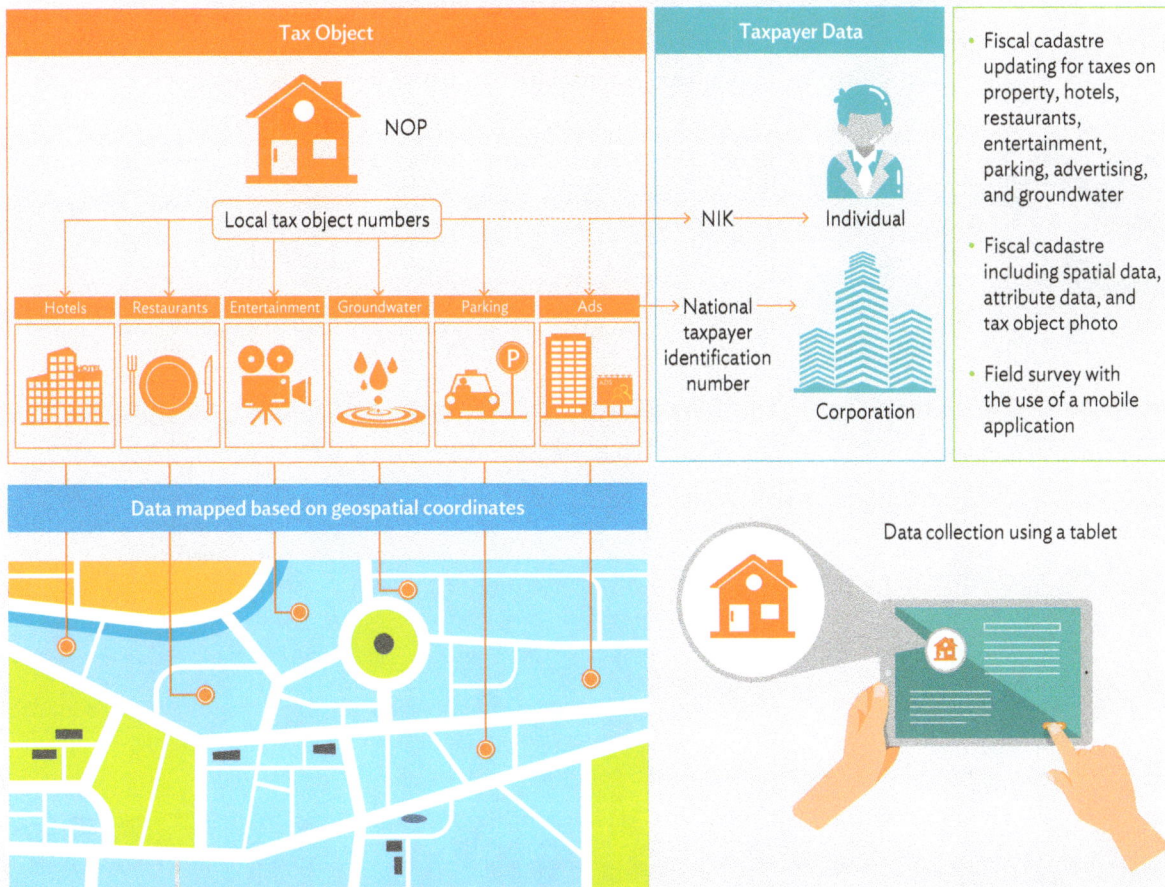

NIK = single identity number, NOP = property identification number, TRAMPIL = Tax Revenue Administration Modernization and Policy Improvement in Local Governments.
Source: Asian Development Bank, TRAMPIL project.

Integrated fiscal cadastre updating of tax objects goes beyond merely recording details about real estate, such as land and buildings. While the main emphasis of TRAMPIL assistance to the pilot local governments involved the implementation of open-source property survey platforms, drones and other technologies were used to map out land and buildings and to update attribute data concerning physical aspects of the properties. Also, further details were recorded on how the mapped properties were being used. Figure 11 contrasts the data-collection process adopted by TRAMPIL with that adopted by the pilot local governments.

The capture of adequate details enables the cadastres to be used to enforce self-assessed taxes on hotels, restaurants, entertainment venues, parking lots, advertising material, and groundwater sites because the comprehensive fiscal cadastre data identify the land and buildings that these entities occupy. Data capture extends to the number and types of rooms and room rates at hotels and the number of tables and chairs in restaurants and their operating hours. In summary, Table 2 highlights how this wider data capture can be achieved efficiently using TRAMPIL methodology, in contrast with existing local government practice.

Figure 11: Local Governments and TRAMPIL Data-Collection Processes

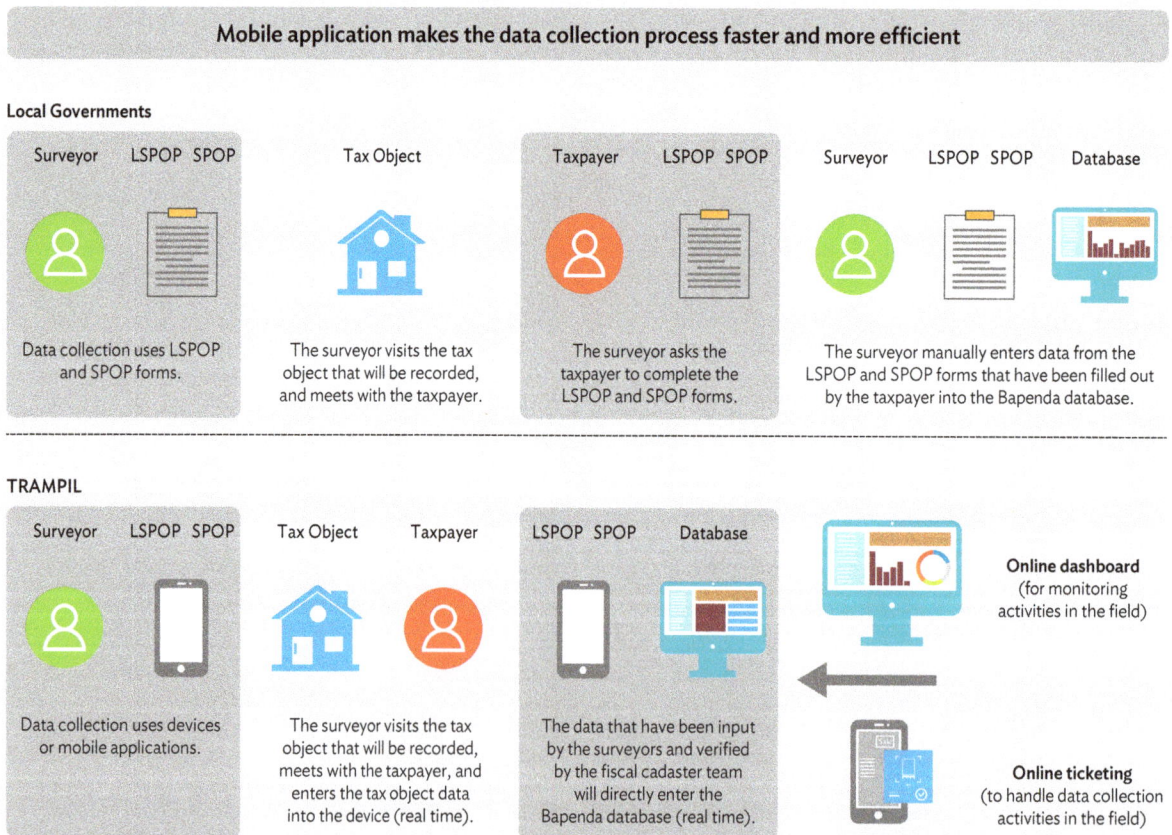

Mobile application makes the data collection process faster and more efficient

Local Governments

| Surveyor LSPOP SPOP | Tax Object | Taxpayer LSPOP SPOP | Surveyor LSPOP SPOP Database |
| Data collection uses LSPOP and SPOP forms. | The surveyor visits the tax object that will be recorded, and meets with the taxpayer. | The surveyor asks the taxpayer to complete the LSPOP and SPOP forms. | The surveyor manually enters data from the LSPOP and SPOP forms that have been filled out by the taxpayer into the Bapenda database. |

TRAMPIL

| Surveyor LSPOP SPOP | Tax Object Taxpayer | LSPOP SPOP Database | |
| Data collection uses devices or mobile applications. | The surveyor visits the tax object that will be recorded, meets with the taxpayer, and enters the tax object data into the device (real time). | The data that have been input by the surveyors and verified by the fiscal cadaster team will directly enter the Bapenda database (real time). | **Online dashboard** (for monitoring activities in the field) **Online ticketing** (to handle data collection activities in the field) |

Bapenda = Regional Revenue Agency, LSPOP = attachment to tax object notification letter, SPOP = tax object notification letter, TRAMPIL = Tax Revenue Administration Modernization and Policy Improvement in Local Governments.

Source: Asian Development Bank, TRAMPIL project.

TRAMPIL technical assistance to the pilot local governments incorporated training in comprehensive fiscal cadastre updating, including data collection planning through mapping and field surveys, quality control over collected data, training in fiscal cadastre mobile applications, the production of a fiscal cadastre technical manual, and supervisory support—all intended to enable local governments to collect fiscal cadastre data independently. To appreciate the magnitude of this aspect of the TRAMPIL technical assistance, it should be noted that some 600 new surveyors in DKI Jakarta received training and other support under the project.

TRAMPIL support for the pilot local governments' capacity to undertake detailed property surveys yielded substantial increases in the number of tax objects recorded, and thus in potential additional PBB-P2 revenue. Two examples illustrate the point.

First, in 2016 and 2017, TRAMPIL helped three pilot local governments—DKI Jakarta, Balikpapan, and Badung—update fiscal cadastres in selected wards, or *kelurahan* (urban wards).[41] Table 3 shows the number of tax objects recorded and the estimated potential additional revenue from the selected *kelurahan*.

Table 3: **Tax Objects and Estimated Potential Additional Revenue in the Pilot Local Governments**

Local Government	Number of *Kelurahan* Surveyed	Total Number of *Kelurahan*	Percentage of *Kelurahan* Surveyed	Number of Tax Objects Surveyed	Estimated Additional Potential Revenue in *Kelurahan* Surveyed (Rp)
DKI Jakarta	6	267	2.2	33,047	180,928,810,699
Balikpapan	4	34	11.8	16,621	11,866,277,666
Badung	5	16	31.3	8,572	544,945,095,750

DKI = Special Capital Region.
Note: *Kelurahan* are urban wards.
Source: ADB. 2020. TRAMPIL Final Report. Jakarta. Unpublished.

It would be simplistic to linearly extrapolate from these survey results conclusions about the potential revenue derivable from all *kelurahan* in the three pilot local governments, as they are not homogenous and those surveyed are not representative. Anecdotally, though, the estimated potential revenue attainable from the surveyed *kelurahan* does point strongly to an opportunity for local governments to significantly augment their local-source revenue by deepening their fiscal cadastre databases through an improved capture of tax objects.

Second, in 2019, TRAMPIL helped update the valuation of high-rise buildings across DKI Jakarta and to assess the value of certain mid-rise buildings. An adoption of the amended or new values for the 586 evaluated tax objects could increase DKI Jakarta's PBB-P2 collection by more than Rp200 billion.

---

[41] The selection favored rapidly expanding *kelurahan* and those with large amounts of taxes in arrears, as well as, in Badung, those with high potential for hotel and restaurant tax collection. The selection of DKI Jakarta locations also took into account potentially high-yielding *kelurahan* in the central business district.

To help local governments comprehensively update their fiscal cadastres, TRAMPIL compiled a property valuation manual that was recommended to be issued by the DGFB through the proposed TRAMPIL website,[42] as a guide for determining the tax object sales values to which the local government-determined PBB-P2 rates must be applied. It is critical that the property-valuation methodology be transparent and equitably applied.

Other positive outcomes of the TRAMPIL project's integrated fiscal cadastre work in the pilot local governments included the following:

(i)   Key stakeholders—such as the heads and secretariats of local governments, the heads of the planning agencies, and the local legislative councils—understand that the fiscal cadastre is the foundation for higher local tax revenue collection, and they know how to collaborate to develop an integrated fiscal cadastre.

(ii)   It was demonstrated that the cost of upgrading a fiscal cadastre is outweighed by the potential increase in tax revenue.

(iii)   LTAs learned better data governance by using a more reliable IT-based data-collection methodology.[43]

(iv)   LTAs improved their capacity to update fiscal cadastres and collect and integrate data.

(v)   Fiscal cadastre surveys were made more cost-efficient by incorporating the full range of local tax objects in each survey.

One consequence of these outcomes was that DKI Jakarta committed to systematically modernizing its tax administration at a cost from its own resources of Rp86.5 billion by the end of 2020, including updating the data on all fiscal cadastre tax objects in DKI Jakarta's 44 *kecamatan*. However, this could not be completed on time due to the coronavirus disease (COVID-19) pandemic. DKI Jakarta also aims to upgrade its core tax IT systems under a separate budget. Similarly, the Balikpapan Tax and Retribution Management Agency included Rp2.1 billion in its budget for 2019 to update its fiscal cadastre for 10 *kelurahan,* using the TRAMPIL methodology and a dedicated team trained by TRAMPIL.

Tax Collection

When the PBB-P2 was transferred from the central government to the local governments in 2010–2014, many tax assessments issued to taxpayers by the central government remained outstanding. However, many of the assessments were based on outdated SISMIOP data, rendering doubtful the tax arrears data inherited by local governments.

Local government indecision and inaction over these arrears have allowed them to continue accumulating since 2010–2014. Now they need to be either collected or written off. To a large extent, the buildup has been attributable to the risk of corruption charges that were rightly or wrongly directed against tax officers who write off tax debt.

---

[42]   See the "TRAMPIL Website" section.

[43]   Data governance and other data issues are discussed in the "Information Technology Development" and "Information Technology Deficiencies" sections.

To guide local governments, TRAMPIL developed a draft manual on how to collect tax arrears, and on tax collection methodology in general. It set out systematic procedures for managing tax receivables, including collection processes and debt write-off rules. To establish consistent treatment across the country, it was recommended that, upon the DGFB's review, the manual and guidance would be issued by the DGFB through the proposed TRAMPIL website.

Local Tax Administration Organization and Business Processes

Traditionally, LTAs have been structured by tax type, with staff divided into teams that specialize in assessing and collecting different kinds of taxes, with little or no cross-interactions among the teams. Modern international tax administration practice adopts a more effective function-based approach that focuses on the taxpayer and on the goal of maximal collection of *all* types of tax revenue from each taxpayer, rather than leaving particular tax office units to deal with only a specific tax type in isolation.

The benefits of a function-based organization are very apparent when, for example, a taxpayer liable for various types of taxes is audited. Where an LTA is organized by tax type, an auditor from one unit examines taxpayer compliance with respect to only that tax type, inefficiently ignoring all others.

The function-based organizational structure in modern tax administrations is normally based on a large taxpayer office (LTO), which has a higher ratio of staff-to-taxpayers than in taxation offices in general. The staff members, who are usually more highly qualified than other tax administration staff, are typically allocated a portfolio of large taxpayers, with whom they liaise directly on all aspects of their tax affairs.

The rationale behind establishing separate LTOs is based on the 20:80 guideline, which states the rule of thumb that 20% of taxpayers pay 80% of the taxes collected. Tax administrations should thus concentrate their highest-quality resources on that highly liable 20% as taxes uncollected from them will hit government coffers harder than uncollected taxes from smaller taxpayers.

The benefits of such specialist units have been evaluated in Indonesia. Box 2 cites a study of the additional tax revenue garnered by the Directorate General of Taxation as a result of the formation of special tax offices with high ratios of staff-to-taxpayers. Although the study concerned corporate taxes and medium-sized taxpayer offices (MTOs), the results have informed local government tax administration practice, as the tax collection gains were attributable to increased declarations of sales revenue, which is the basis of local government self-assessment taxes. In effect, the increased tax revenue did not arise from increased tax collection efforts, but from greater and sustained formalization. Consequently, the results of the research point to the potential advantage of LTAs, in particular those in larger local governments, establishing LTOs (and perhaps MTOs, too, in the case of the very large LTAs, such as DKI Jakarta) to ensure full compliance by larger self-assessing taxpayers.

Box 2: Empirical Study of Special Taxpayer Offices in Indonesia

Basri et al. (2019) found that "the introduction of... enhanced tax administration via the MTOs dramatically increased tax revenue. Real total taxes paid [by] affected taxpayers increased by 128 percent... that is, moving firms to the MTOs more than *doubled* (emphasis in the original) average tax collections from these firms over the subsequent six years. The government's increased costs of administering taxes through the MTOs were minuscule—less than 1 percent of the additional revenue collected—so the net increase in government revenue is almost identical to the gross increase. All types of taxes paid by these firms rose dramatically...

"The transition to improved tax administration—characterized by higher staff-to-taxpayer ratios—led to substantially higher tax revenues. This came in the form of higher top-line revenues being reported by firms, rather than decreased deductions or changes in the degree to which taxes due were collected. The increases in tax revenues for the government were more than two orders of magnitude larger than the increases in administrative costs associated with the increased enforcement...

"[I]mproved tax administration dramatically increased net government revenues and encouraged formalization.

"In short, our results suggest that meaningfully large increases in tax revenue for medium-sized firms can be obtained through feasible administrative improvements in a relatively short period of time, and that the potential gains from these types of policies are large relative to tax rate changes."

The authors noted that marginal corporate income tax rates on MTO taxpayers would have had to be increased by 23 percentage points, or about 6 percentage points across all firms, to raise the same amount of revenue that the government obtained by improving tax administration.

Moreover, they found that the tax revenue from MTO taxpayers "*grows* (emphasis in the original), not shrinks, over time: the effects of the MTO on taxes paid and on reported gross incomes 6 years after firms were transferred into the MTO were between 1.5 and 2.5 times larger than they were 2 years after being moved to the MTO, despite the fact that staffing levels and enforcement actions from the MTO... remained essentially constant over time...

"[T]he dramatic increases in reported tax revenue from MTO firms over time come not from increased effectiveness of the MTO at collecting taxes due... but rather that MTO firms reported substantially higher revenues to the government over time...

"Given these estimates, improved tax administration is likely to be the preferred approach unless the compliance costs imposed on taxpayers are extremely high."

MTO = medium-sized taxpayer office.
Source: M. C. Basri et al. 2019. Tax Administration vs. Tax Rates: Evidence from Corporate Taxation in Indonesia. *NBER Working Paper Series*. No. 26150. Cambridge MA: National Bureau of Economic Research. https://www.nber.org/system/files/working_papers/w26150/w26150.pdf.

One implication for local governments, according to a study by Basri et al. (2019) is that "firms report substantially more sales once they move to the MTO... [T]he main mechanism through which improved tax administration led to increased revenue is through capturing more top-line business activity."[44] This is particularly important for local governments as their self-assessed taxes on commercial activity are all based on sales.

The findings of the study are particularly pertinent to the larger cities in Indonesia.

---

[44]   M. C. Basri et al. 2019. Tax Administration vs. Tax Rates: Evidence from Corporate Taxation in Indonesia. *NBER Working Paper Series*. No. 26150. Cambridge, MA: National Bureau of Economic Research. p. 22. https://www.nber.org/system/files/working_papers/w26150/w26150.pdf.

Over 145 countries, or nearly two-thirds of the global total, are less populous than DKI Jakarta alone, and the tax administrations of many of these countries have LTOs. Seventy-three countries, some of them with LTOs, are less populous than even the 12th-largest city in Indonesia. Thus, ample precedent justifies a consideration of the formation of LTOs by Indonesia's larger cities to enhance revenue collection from the major contributors of local government revenue and the taxation services they receive.

TRAMPIL drafted a guide on tax administration to promote the adoption of the function-based organization of LTAs and provide references to help local governments design and implement processes to improve LTA performance. It also compiled a business process design manual for developing core tax functions. When transitioning to a function-based organization structure, each LTA needs to assess its readiness, particularly in terms of human resources, and it needs a transition plan.

In addition, TRAMPIL introduced the Performance Indicator Standard for Local Tax Administration (SIKAP), a diagnostic tool that enables local governments to self-assess their capacity to carry out their assigned functions.

On the enhancement of human resource skills, TRAMPIL compiled the *Human Capital Management and Change Management Manual* and conducted employee engagement and perception surveys in the DKI Jakarta, Badung, and Balikpapan LTAs. The surveys revealed the need to improve service delivery and IT systems. Taxpayer satisfaction and perception surveys were carried out in Badung and Balikpapan to provide input into a taxpayer satisfaction index to measure the progress of improvement in each LTA.

Information Technology Development

TRAMPIL work on fiscal cadastres, as discussed in the "Development of Comprehensive Fiscal Cadastre Databases" section, pointed to the need for sophisticated core IT systems in local governments. The broad concept of an integrated core tax-administration IT system is illustrated in Figure 12.

The fiscal cadastre data information system is a subsystem of a local government's wider IT system. Local governments need an integrated IT system that draws on information gathered in one subsystem to perform actions driven by another part of the IT system. For example, to issue tax assessments, the assessment-issuing processes of the IT system should integrate with taxpayer registration and fiscal cadastre components. This integration around a core IT system is a fundamental feature of modern tax administration. TRAMPIL, thus, helped DKI Jakarta to improve its data management by integrating its population, land, property, spatial, and demographic data; tax and retribution data; water usage data; and social data into a single data information system that is accessible to all relevant work units.

To help local governments upgrade their IT systems, TRAMPIL developed medium-term IT blueprints, both general and specific, for the four pilot governments. The blueprints are based on IT gap analyses, which generated recommendations for system design and road maps for implementation. Box 3 describes the IT developments in the Balikpapan and Bandung pilot LTAs.

Figure 12: Integrated Core Tax-Administration Information Technology System

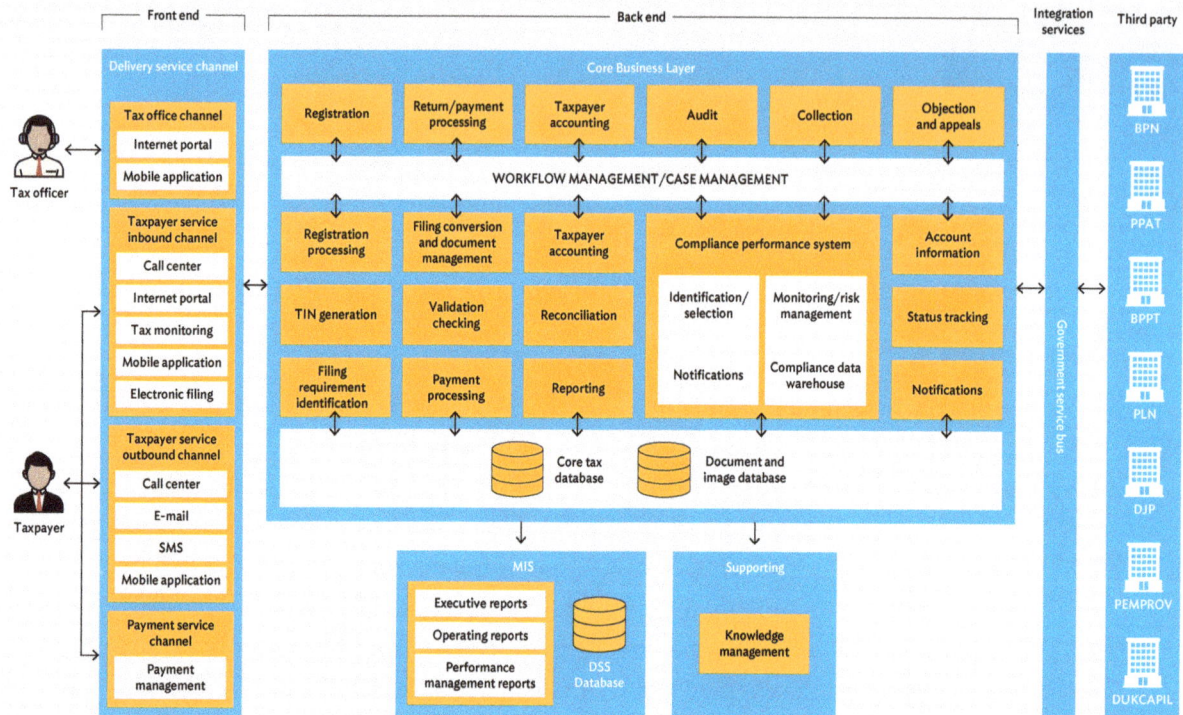

BPN = National Land Agency, BPPT = Agency for Assessment and Application of Technology, DGT = Directorate General of Taxation, DSS = decision support system, Dukcapil = Department of Population and Civil Registration, MIS = management information system, Pemprov = provincial government, PLN = state electricity firm, PPAT = land deed official, SMS = short message service, TIN = tele-electronic identification number.

Source: Asian Development Bank, Tax Revenue Administration Modernization and Policy Improvement in Local Governments project.

Box 3: Information Technology Development in Balikpapan and Bandung

Local governments used TRAMPIL IT gap analysis as a guide for planning their IT system investments and budgets, as well as their IT development and implementation.

Balikpapan allocated a budget for IT development based on TRAMPIL's IT blueprint and gap analysis. The main finding on the use of ICT in Balikpapan was a lack of ICT experts that are able to carry out system design and maintenance. Balikpapan engaged only one temporary employee to perform these tasks. Overall, IT development suffered from poor management and a lack of planning. This is clearly not an ideal way to manage ICT.

In Bandung, the main finding was a lack of user involvement in determining system requirements. Consequently, the IT system did not meet user needs. Before the IT gap analysis was conducted, two departments—the IT self-assessment team and the IT official assessment team—used their own separate systems, with no collaboration on IT development. This approach generated divergent standards without system or data integration.

IT gap analysis enabled both IT departments to combine and integrate their data. To facilitate data integration, they requested project support from TRAMPIL, beginning with the migration of property tax data into similar databases for other tax types.

ICT = information and communication technology, IT = information technology, TRAMPIL = Tax Revenue Administration Modernization and Policy Improvement in Local Governments.

Source: Asian Development Bank, TRAMPIL project.

To ensure the integrity of data used to assess taxes in DKI Jakarta, TRAMPIL, as part of the Jakarta Satu, or "one policy, one data, one map," initiative, helped DKI Jakarta make its Communication and Information Agency the central administrator of tax data and applications, rendering DKI Jakarta's regional tax and levies agency the only user of the data and applications.

Box 4 summarizes the key TRAMPIL achievements in local government tax administration.

Box 4: Key TRAMPIL Achievements in Local Tax Administration

(i)   Assistance and supervisory support provided to pilot LTAs for the following purposes:
    a.   incorporating more comprehensive and accurate coverage of property and ownership data in fiscal cadastres,
    b.   spatial mapping of land and buildings using drone and other mobile technologies,
    c.   updating physical property attributes data in fiscal cadastres,
    d.   implementing open-source fiscal cadastre property survey platforms, and
    e.   updating fiscal cadastre valuations for both general tax object categories and specific tax objects;

(ii)   Carried out IT gap analyses in the four pilot local governments;

(iii)   Developed medium-term IT blueprints, both general and specific, for the four pilot local governments;

(iv)   Triggered DKI Jakarta's introduction of Jakarta Satu;

(v)   Achieved the production of
    a.   a fiscal cadastre technical manual,
    b.   a property valuation manual,
    c.   a manual on collecting tax payments in arrears,
    d.   an academic paper reviewing and proposing a strategy to improve tax collection,
    e.   a guide on tax-administration organizational structure and processes,
    f.   a business process design manual,
    g.   a manual on human capital management and change management,
    h.   an employee engagement survey manual,
    i.   a taxpayer satisfaction survey manual,
    j.   a SIKAP diagnostic tool,
    k.   TRAMPIL website user manuals, and
    l.   a concept note on registering and taxing tourist accommodation providers using online booking platforms;

(vi)   Developed the TRAMPIL website;

(vii)   Conducted training workshops on
    a.   fiscal cadastre updating,
    b.   collecting tax arrears,
    c.   tax administration processes,
    d.   SIKAP, and
    e.   the TRAMPIL website; and

(viii) Helped pilot LTAs to conduct
    a.   employee engagement and perception surveys (in DKI Jakarta, Badung, and Balikpapan), and
    b.   taxpayer satisfaction and perception surveys (in Badung and Balikpapan).

DKI = Special Capital Region, IT = information technology, LTA = local tax administration, SIKAP = Performance Indicator Standard for Local Tax Administration, TRAMPIL = Tax Revenue Administration Modernization and Policy Improvement in Local Governments.
Source: Asian Development Bank, TRAMPIL project.

Challenges for TRAMPIL Pilot Local Governments

TRAMPIL support for the four pilot local governments undoubtedly produced positive outcomes, but it also revealed a broad range of challenges involved in the accomplishment of greater local-source revenue mobilization. The two most profound constraints observed in the pilot regions were (i) a low commitment to reform and (ii) very significant constraints on local government capacity to implement reform. These and other impediments are examined below.

Commitment to Local Government Tax Reform

To ensure the success of the local government tax-modernization program, key stakeholders needed to be strongly committed to it. In fact, local governments differed in their degree of commitment, and this significantly affected progress. Factors included frequent changes in leadership, the prioritization of short-term revenue targets over improving fundamental aspects of tax administration for more sustainable revenue gains over the long term, reluctance to take ownership of reform, and low employee engagement.[45]

To resolve the lack of commitment, it is important for central government agencies, in particular the Directorate General of Fiscal Balance (DGFB) and the Ministry of Home Affairs (MOHA), to maintain communication and coordination with the local government leadership; ensure its ongoing commitment; and clarify for local government management the need to commit to reform, enunciating the benefits for the community and for the local government itself. It would also be beneficial to realize specified capacity-building goals and the benefits of the tax-modernization program in terms of revenue increases and improvements in taxpayer compliance within the term of each head of local government.[46] Further, senior local government managers need to instruct staff to commit to reform, and to impress upon them the benefits for the community, local government, and ultimately themselves.

However, implementing this approach is hampered by MOHA regulations concerning the conditions of employment, which are applicable to personnel in all government agencies. As discussed below, this barrier can be overcome only by coordinating policy reform across central government ministries.

---

[45] The DKI Jakarta employee engagement survey in the "Local Tax Administration Organization and Business Processes" section found that based on a survey response rate of 98%, employee engagement turned out to be below the minimum standard. Moreover, 8 of 14 factors were below minimum standards: leadership, recognition, opportunity to grow, remuneration, clear direction, resources, customer service culture, and employee commitment.

[46] Staff rotation is addressed in more detail in the next section.

Human Capacity Limitations

As with commitment, there is marked variation in the capacity of different local governments across Indonesia to implement local revenue mobilization. At one extreme, DKI Jakarta suffers relatively few capacity constraints, as it is the country's most prosperous local government and the best located for attracting qualified human resources to undertake implementation. Many other regions, especially the poorer ones, suffer fiscal deficits and a paucity of skilled human resources.

The uneven abilities of different regions to attract suitably qualified personnel necessitates the use of incentives to attract people to less appealing regions. This requires that local governments be allowed greater flexibility in hiring employees. Leveling the playing field will require two things:

(i)   a liaison between the DGFB and MOHA, as the problem spans the jurisdiction of both central government agencies;[47] and

(ii) additional central government contributions from the special allocation fund (DAK) to those regions that need skilled personnel but lack sufficient financial resources to fund the incentives required to attract them.

Indonesian government bodies suffer from very frequent and seemingly uncoordinated staff rotations, which has had a significant impact on the local government tax-modernization program, at both the central and local levels. These rotations cause regular losses of skills, experience, and institutional knowledge. In all the pilots, the frequent changes in leadership, especially when they involved the replacement of the head of the local government or the head of the LTA, undermined the smooth implementation of reform. Knowledge transfer was poor when the staff rotated.

Successful local government tax reform, therefore, requires lesser staff rotations, as well as the introduction of formal knowledge-transfer procedures, to be applied when staff rotations do occur. In local governments, a bare minimum of staff needs to be retained over the medium term to allow skills to accrue in positions that are critical to the reform program in LTAs, particularly in auditing, valuation, and arrears collection. Tempering the frequency of staff rotations will require an agreement between the DGFB and MOHA to amend the relevant regulations.

Businesses complain that local government tax personnel lack an understanding of their tax affairs. This deficiency clearly constrains efficient service delivery, and points to the need for intensive training to lift the technical expertise of the staff enough to allow an LTA to carry out its functions better and to empower the self-improvement of individual staff members. Plainly, differences in the capacities of different regions to implement the central government's proposed reforms need to be taken into account when setting expectations for each local government's achievements. This is particularly relevant to the design of a rollout strategy discussed in Chapter 5.

---

[47] This liaison may well require initiation at the ministerial or even presidential level.

Lack of Comprehensive Fiscal Cadastre Databases

The benefits and international popularity of local government property taxes were discussed in the section on "Development of Comprehensive Fiscal Cadastre Databases." Despite the merits of property taxes, however, Indonesia collects relatively little of them by international standards. Considerable potential revenue from this source remains unexploited because local government fiscal cadastres are neither complete nor comprehensive.[48] Rural areas present a particular need for the identification of property rights, which are often unclear.

A fully comprehensive updating of local government fiscal cadastres is a good starting point for immediately improving local-source tax revenue. Data gathering and updating is, therefore, required to complete the fiscal cadastres and bring extant information up to date. That involves verifying tax objects through surveys and accurately categorizing the collected tax object data to minimize errors and thereby maximize tax potential.

TRAMPIL activities to enhance fiscal cadastre databases in the pilot local governments, as summarized in the section titled "Success Achieved by TRAMPIL in Pilot Local Governments," revealed that part of the reason for incomplete fiscal cadastres is inability to gain access to the properties for surveys, either because the owners were absent or entry was barred by the owners or their security personnel. This highlights the need for statutory powers, where lacking, to guarantee access to properties and to enforce appropriate sanctions in cases of noncompliance.[49] Coupled with this is the need for local governments to embark on targeted and thorough socialization programs to raise public awareness of the purpose of fiscal cadastre surveys and how they are conducted. There is considerable scope for further coordinated external technical assistance for fiscal cadastre updating, including training.

Information Technology Deficiencies

Two common problems are weak data governance in LTAs and the poor integration of information systems into a single core tax IT system.[50] Also lacking is online filing of self-assessment returns, which is now standard practice in modern tax administrations. Movement toward integrated IT functions and electronic service delivery to local government taxpayers will be necessary to improve efficiency and, thus, the financial position of local governments. This would require the provision of adequate financial and other resources to invest in additional hardware, as well as qualified personnel to deliver appropriate IT solutions. Again, additional central government funding will be necessary for investments in poorer regions.[51]

---

[48] "The cadastral system in Indonesia covers only 35 per cent of the country, mainly in the urban areas of the island of Java." L. Caripis. 2017. *Combatting Corruption in Mining Approvals: Assessing the Risks in 18 Resource-Rich Countries.* Sydney: Transparency International. p. 38. https://www.extractiveshub.org/servefile/getFile/id/6675.

[49] The proposed amendments to Law 28/2009 do not provide these powers to surveyors gathering fiscal cadastre information.

[50] This system is described in the section titled "Information Technology Development."

[51] The potential economies of scale obtainable from the standardization of local government ICT solutions, especially those funded by the central government, are examples of efficiency gains from rationalization, referred to in the "Policy Achievements under TRAMPIL" section.

Proper data governance is a fundamental requirement of a modern LTA. It enables an organization to ensure that high data quality is maintained throughout the complete data life cycle. This means maintaining the integrity of data availability, usability, consistency, and security. On security, none of the pilot LTAs had comprehensive protocols in place to counter cyber attacks or disasters, which could have destroyed their databases. Cloud computing options should be considered as methods of resolving this shortcoming.

Appropriate data governance requires policies and procedures, compliance and enforcement, and staff capacity to ensure effective data management throughout the LTA. Policies and procedures address, for example, accountability for data change (that is, determining who has authority to revise, update, or replace data), the processes for changing data, internal control, and documentation.

To improve control over the quality of data, a clear separation is necessary between those people who administer data and those who own and use it. Here, too, the four pilot local governments had weak data management, with tax data and applications fully administered by each local tax office. Particularly in this age of concern for the protection of personal data, segregation between data administrators and data users, as is done in DKI Jakarta (described in the "Information Technology Development" section), needs to be implemented in other local governments to ensure the privacy of the data they hold. Having ensured the integrity of the data, governments need to strengthen user analysis of the data to achieve better-informed policy formulation.

Complexity of Local Government Tax Administration

Chapter 2 emphasized the central government's core economic policy of attracting investment to enable economic growth in Indonesia. Businesses claim that decentralization has increased compliance costs for taxpayers and administrative costs for tax assessment and collection, especially for self-assessed taxes on taxable sales of goods and services. The tax regime is generally perceived as contradictory and inconsistently enforced, giving rise to business uncertainty.[52] Investors express similar concerns about Indonesia's regulatory environment.[53] These criticisms are directed at both the central and local government tax regimes. The upshot of these allegations is a perception on the part of businesses and investors that Indonesia has an antibusiness climate.

If the central government's core economic policy of encouraging investment and growth is to succeed, local governments and relevant central government agencies need to ensure that new tax and regulatory measures militate against increased compliance costs. The tasks required of businesses as they respond to LTAs need to be simplified. The mantra in countries that have been successful in this respect is that, as far as practicable, businesses should spend their time doing what they do best, which is running their business, rather than being burdened with extra downtime due to unnecessary tax-compliance activities.

---

[52] C. Lewis. 2019. Raising More Public Revenue in Indonesia in a Growth- and Equity-Friendly Way. *OECD Economics Department Working Papers*. No. 1534. Paris: Organisation for Economic Co-operation and Development (OECD). p. 15. https://www.oecd.org/officialdocuments/publicdisplaydocumentpdf/?cote=ECO/WKP(2019)3&docLanguage=En.

[53] Footnote 52, p. 23.

Local government bureaucratic barriers need to be removed.[54] This would clearly entail confronting corruption in local government.

Reform must focus on simplicity and taxpayers' ease of doing business with LTAs.[55]

Tax simplicity means an uncomplicated tax-administration system. It demands a new mindset that recognizes the need for more streamlined local tax and regulatory regimes, to ensure that taxes are easily and efficiently collected, to contain the administrative costs of collection, to contain the cost of compliance for taxpayers, and ensure that their taxes are easily paid. These objectives are achieved by having the LTAs offer electronic services, such as online filing and payment.

The major benefit of an approach that improves the ease of doing business is higher taxpayer compliance. Some observers contend that, in the tourism industry, for example, the administrative burden of tax compliance discourages small operators, in particular, from registering for tax purposes.[56] Moreover, with predictable and transparent behavior by LTA officials, taxpayers can anticipate the consequences of tax decisions with reasonable certainty, which makes their business decisions more reliable.

The prevailing business-licensing system, of which local governments are a part, is an immediate impediment to business and investment (Box 5). Local governments can independently address this issue by (i) determining whether each license requirement is really necessary; and (ii) simplifying the permit-granting process, which would involve limiting the number of procedures or steps required, and thus reducing the time required to issue a license—as demonstrated, for example, by DKI Jakarta's initiative Jakarta Satu.

Noncompliance

Indonesia is notorious for its generally low rate of tax compliance, especially for the underreporting of information required to levy taxes.[57] As with taxes imposed by the central government, increasing local tax compliance is tackled on two fronts: first, by capturing all potential taxpayers in the local government's tax registration database, netting all taxpayers who should be registered, but are not; and, second, by implementing effective means of auditing and enforcement to ensure that taxpayers pay the amount of tax required.

---

[54] The TRAMPIL project itself experienced bureaucratic frustrations similar to those described by Indonesia's business community, as illustrated by two examples. First was the need to obtain multiple permits, from DKI Jakarta, the Ministry of Transportation, and the Air Force, in order to deploy drones for spatial mapping to update the fiscal cadastre. Second was a requirement of obtaining letters of authorization from mayors for training activities conducted by LTAs for heads of districts and members of the community.

[55] Indonesia ranked 73rd of 190 countries in the World Bank 2019 Ease of Doing Business Index. The World Bank. Ease of Doing Business Index. https://data.worldbank.org/indicator/IC.BUS.EASE.XQ?most_recent_value_desc=false.

[56] P. Ollivaud and P. Haxton. 2019. Making the Most of Tourism in Indonesia to Promote Sustainable Regional Development. *OECD Economics Department Working Papers.* No. 1535. Paris: OECD. p. 23. https://www.oecd-ilibrary.org/docserver/c73325d9-en.pdf?expires=1618629990&id=id&accname=guest&checksum=646A063A8C36E4FFF36EF94652A77ABF.

[57] A. Rahman. 2017. *Tax Compliance in Indonesia: The Role of Public Officials as Taxpayers.* PhD dissertation. Enschede, Netherlands: University of Twente. pp. 8, 26, and 118.

Box 5: Business Facilitation, Not Tax

"The problem… is that Indonesia is still notorious for its arduous business licensing procedures. Tax incentives will be meaningless if investors are forced to pay unusually high costs for starting up a business because of the fundamental factors cited… as regulatory and bureaucratic barriers.

"President Joko 'Jokowi' Widodo loudly complained at the Cabinet meeting that he was utterly disappointed with the slow pace of reform in business licensing, notably in the investment and export sectors. Even though Indonesia's rank in the World Bank's Ease of Doing Business Index among 190 countries has risen, we are still among the lowest in the ASEAN region.

"Jokowi's bid to create an online single submission system for the dozens of business permits needed from the central government and regional administrations still faces poor coordination between government agencies.

"National Development Planning Minister Bambang Brodjonegoro also admitted… that regulatory and bureaucratic barriers remain among the main disadvantages for investing in the country."

Source: Editorial Board. 2019. Business Facilitation, Not Tax. *The Jakarta Post*. 21 June. https://www.thejakartapost.com/academia/ 2019/06/21/business-facilitation-not-tax.html.

Both of these tax-compliance strategies are especially relevant for self-assessment business taxpayers.

Compliance with tax obligations often follows from compliance with the underlying obligations. For example, groundwater cannot be legally extracted without a permit (Box 6). Permit issuance constitutes a data point that triggers the imposition of groundwater tax. Consequently, the illegal extraction of groundwater, which may be unknown to the local government because no permit to extract it has ever been issued, deprives the local government of tax revenue because the groundwater tax is self-assessed, dependent on the extractor declaring the amount of groundwater extracted. People who have not obtained permits from their local government to extract groundwater are hardly likely to disclose to the same local government the amount of groundwater extracted. However, once these groundwater extractors start to comply with the underlying obligation to obtain extraction permits, local-source tax revenue increases.[58] Thus, no tax collection is possible as long as taxpayers hide their noncompliance with the law that deals with groundwater extraction itself. To put it simply, if the illegal extraction issue is remedied, the local-source tax revenue base will automatically grow as a secondary benefit. When illegal extraction is discovered, only a lack of supervision and enforcement will prevent the collection of the groundwater tax.

Noncompliance is, in large part, attributable to the existence of a large informal sector in the Indonesian economy. The underreporting problem is accentuated in a self-assessment tax regime, which inherently depends on voluntary compliance. One example is the registration and taxation of tourist accommodation providers that use online reservation platforms. TRAMPIL prepared a concept note on a system to monitor revenue from this source, which is subject to a hotel tax.

---

[58]   In DKI Jakarta, this revenue may even be used to help resolve the problem of land subsidence, in accordance with the benefit principle of taxation (Chapter 4).

Box 6: Jakarta, the Fastest-Sinking City in the World

"[W]hen groundwater is pumped out, the land above it sinks as if it is sitting on a deflating balloon—and this leads to land subsidence.

"The situation is exacerbated by lax regulation allowing just about anyone, from individual homeowners to massive shopping mall operators, to carry out their own groundwater extractions.

"'Everyone has a right, from residents to industries, to use groundwater so long as this is regulated,' says Heri Andreas [lecturer and researcher in Earth science at the Bandung Institute of Technology]. The problem is that they take more than what is allowed.

"People say they have no choice when the authorities are unable to meet their water needs and experts confirm that water management authorities can only meet 40% of Jakarta's demand for water.

"A landlord in central Jakarta, known only as Hendri, runs a dormitory-like block called a *kos-kosan* and has been pumping his own groundwater for 10 years to supply tenants. He is one of many on his street who do this.

"'It's better to use our own groundwater rather than relying on the authorities. A *kos-kosan* like this needs a lot of water.'

"The local government has only recently admitted it has a problem with illegal groundwater extraction.

"In May, the Jakarta city authority inspected 80 buildings in Central Jakarta's Jalan Thamrin, a road lined with skyscrapers, shopping malls and hotels. It found that 56 buildings had their own groundwater pump and 33 were extracting water illegally.

"Jakarta's Governor Anies Baswedan says everyone should have a licence, which will enable the authorities to measure how much groundwater is being extracted. Those without a licence will have their building-worthiness certificate revoked, as would other businesses in the same building."

Source: M. L. Mayuri and R. Hidayat. 2018. Jakarta, the Fastest-Sinking City in the World. *BBC News Indonesia*. 13 August. https://www.bbc.com/news/world-asia-44636934.

In addition to encouraging voluntary compliance by means of public awareness (or public information) campaigns, including through social media, and implementing sanctions for noncompliance, the government could achieve greater tax compliance by strengthening local government capacity and efforts to monitor compliance, thus, improving the odds that a noncompliant taxpayer will be discovered and made to pay the taxes owed, together with penalties for noncompliance.

Noncompliant taxpayers are found predominantly through tax audits. For local governments, this means developing the capacity of their tax auditors to plan and conduct thorough and systematic audits on a functional basis, auditing for all local taxes for which a taxpayer is liable; and evaluating the outcomes of those audits.

One of the features of the Indonesian tax system is that the same taxpayer is typically subject to both central and local taxes, which are levied on overlapping tax bases. For example, self-assessment taxpayers like hotel and restaurant operators are subject to a hotel or restaurant tax levied by local governments, and to the income tax, which is levied by the central government. The correct assessment of both local and central taxes relies on the disclosure of accurately recorded sales revenue—gross sales revenue for the hotel or restaurant tax; and, for the income tax, net sales revenue after expenses are deducted.

Omitted sales, which reduce the collections of local self-assessed taxes, also reduce the central government's corporate and personal income tax revenues.

When a taxpayer's local government taxes and income tax are independently audited, as they currently are, sales revenue is audited twice by the separate taxing authorities. That increases taxpayers' compliance costs; and this is inefficient from a tax-administration viewpoint, particularly if one is seeking to benefit the whole of government by improving efficiency in the delivery of public services.

Duplication of effort and cost can be combatted by having the LTAs and the Directorate General of Taxation (DGT) conduct their audits jointly. Under such circumstances, LTA auditors could concentrate on auditing sales revenue, thereby developing technical expertise in this area and saving DGT audit costs. DGT auditors would defer to this expertise and use for income-tax purposes the information and outcomes of the LTA-conducted revenue section of the audit.

Audits of taxpayers' expenses, which are critical to the correct assessment of their income tax liability, fall within the purview of the DGT. LTA auditors would, therefore, defer to DGT audits of expenses, as the LTAs are not directly concerned with them. However, a taxpayer's expenses can provide valuable information to LTA auditors, not about the audited taxpayer, but about the other taxpayers who have received payments from the audited taxpayer—income that may well be subject to local taxes. Therefore, certain information gleaned from a DGT audit of a taxpayer's expenses may be useful to LTA auditors.

To ensure the collection of the correct amount of local taxes from taxpayers, DGT audit information that is relevant and helpful to LTA auditors should be made available to them. The exchange of audit information between the local governments and the DGT would be beneficial to both taxing authorities. The outcome of this sort of coordination and cooperation between LTA and DGT audits would take the country as a whole toward the goal of enabling both the central and local governments to collect the correct amount of taxes.

For the same reasons, information exchange between local governments is also important. Many self-assessment taxpayers conduct business across more than one local government jurisdiction and interact with other businesses within each jurisdiction. The same benefits of communication between the central and local governments would also apply to communication among local governments. Again, the local-source tax revenues of multiple local governments could be enhanced by joint audits and the exchange of taxpayer information.

Noncompliance is detected not just from audits of revenues and expenses. Evidence of noncompliance arises from numerous sources, which, in line with international practice, increasingly requires broader leeway to allow tax officials to obtain data from third parties with which a taxpayer interacts, such as banks for a taxpayer's bank account information and movement of funds. Moreover, information exchange between a local government and the DGT about taxpayers could come about because, on the one hand, LTAs have greater local knowledge than the DGT and, on the other, the DGT has a larger database on taxpayers, including internationally sourced information. The sharing of knowledge on a taxpayer that does not necessarily arise from an audit would also be beneficial to both tax agencies.

Seamless knowledge sharing and joint auditing would be enhanced by harmonizing tax identification numbers and registration information through, for example, a common record of a taxpayer's bank accounts lodged at the time of taxpayer registration with either the DGT or a local government. The simplified case study example in Box 7, which is drawn from a typical international tax-avoidance arrangement, illustrates how information obtained and used by the DGT for one tax can enhance local tax collection when shared with the relevant local government.

The sort of cooperation illustrated in Box 7 would ensure that tax collection is optimized across the whole government, and that the tax base is consistent, regardless of the type of tax being levied. Further, the increased hotel tax revenue that could have been collected by the Denpasar LTA as a result of information received from the DGT would have reduced the fiscal pressure on the central government, which could then, in turn, reduce the transfers from the general allocation fund (DAU) to fill the fiscal gap of the Denpasar local government.

Box 7: Case Study: Sharing International Hotel Revenue Information to Increase Hotel Tax Collections

A resident Indonesian company, IComp, which is a member of a multinational hotel group, operates a luxury hotel in Bali. It sells a block of rooms on a full-board basis for $300 per room per night to a travel wholesale company called WComp, which is also a member of the group and is based in the Cayman Islands. WComp on-sells the rooms to independent distributors and travel agents in Japan for $800 per night. After adding their profit margin, the independent distributors and travel agents sell the rooms to end-users for an average price of $900 per night. This arrangement enables WComp's $500 profit to be made in the Cayman Islands, where the company is not required to pay any tax on it.[a]

IComp declares a revenue of Rp4,212,000 per room per night ($300 at Rp14,040 per dollar[b]) to the DGT for income tax purposes and to the Denpasar LTA for hotel tax purposes. It pays the Denpasar LTA a hotel tax of Rp421,200 per room per night sold (10% of Rp4,212,000).

The transfer pricing division of the DGT becomes aware of this arrangement through an international exchange of information as agreed between Indonesia and the country of residence of IComp's parent company. It makes transfer pricing adjustments that increase IComp's revenue for income tax purposes to Rp10,530,000 (or $750) per room per night. However, the Denpasar LTA is unaware of the DGT adjustment.

In this case, information sharing between the DGT and the Denpasar LTA would have enabled the LTA to increase its local-source hotel tax revenue by Rp631,800 per room per night—from Rp421,200 to Rp1,053,000, per room per night (10% of ([$750 – $300] x Rp14,040))—as Article 34 of Law No. 28 of 2009 on local taxes and charges allows a local government to impose a hotel tax on "the total payment *or the amount that should be paid to the hotel*" (emphasis added).[c]

DGT = Directorate General of Taxation, LTA = local tax administration, Rp = Indonesian rupiah.

[a] The large gross profit margin here is arguably justified by WComp based on the argument that it owns or must pay for the intellectual property and shared resources of the multinational hotel group, including its brand(s), standard international operating systems, worldwide reservations system, customer loyalty program, etc.

[b] This is assumed the be the rupiah–dollar exchange rate.

[c] From a policy perspective, the language of Article 34 should be tightened to remove the debatable ambiguity of the words "should be paid." Instead, an objective determination of the relevant amount should be explicitly stated. For instance, it could be the application of the average rate advertised on the hotel's website to the applicable date(s).

Source: TRAMPIL.

This holistic approach to assessing taxes for the mutual benefit of the central and local governments extends to taxes that are not self-assessed. To capture their full potential tax revenue, local governments have a vested interest in DGT enforcement of national taxes, part of which are allocated to the local governments through the revenue sharing fund (DBH). For example, the central and local governments have an overlapping interest in personal income tax (PIT) assessment because the central government is required to allocate 20% of the collected tax revenue to the local governments in whose jurisdiction the PIT taxpayers reside (or, under the proposed amendments to Law 28/2009, the central government would be entitled to the base amount of PIT revenues, while local governments would be entitled to a surcharge on it).

To illustrate this point, a local government may have information that is relevant to a taxpayer's PIT liability, which was gleaned from sales information obtained by the local government in the course of examining, for example, the taxpayer's restaurant tax returns. Clearly, this should be shared with the DGT to ensure that the taxpayer pays the correct amount of PIT, to the benefit of both levels of government. Therefore, cooperation and information sharing between local governments and the central government—ideally automated through information and communication technology (ICT)—is necessary to ensure maximum PIT collection by the DGT.

The proposed amendments to Law 28/2009 gave broad powers that are intended to facilitate information exchange. Article 153(1) provided that "the agency authorized to collect taxes and Head of Region can exchange data and information" toward assessing taxes.[59] To avoid legislative conflict, this broad, straightforward provision should trigger the repeal of the more restrictive Article 34 of Law 6/1983, as amended, concerning general taxation provisions and procedures, in which Article 34(3) empowers the minister of finance, in the interest of the state, to give written approval to an official to provide information concerning a taxpayer to a party designated by the minister. Further, para. 2(a) of the elucidation of Article 34 states that the third party to which otherwise confidential taxpayer information can be released is the state institution with authority to conduct an investigation in the context of *state* (i.e., national government) finance. That would seem to preclude audits conducted by local governments, which are in the context of local government finance, not state finance.

More broadly, the laws should be reviewed to raise them to current international data-sharing standards. Consequential legislative amendments must incorporate safeguards to ensure that information that is exchanged is not misused, as is contemplated by Articles 152(1) and 153(2) of the proposed amendments to Law 28/2009. The alignment of Law 28/2009 and Law 6/1983 on information exchange is a further example of the need to adopt a holistic approach to the reform of local government tax administration that demands the cooperation and coordination of central and local government policy makers and legal drafters.

---

[59] The "agency authorized to collect taxes" referred to in the proposed Article 153(1) is presumably the DGT. The wording of this provision should be clarified to encompass other local governments as well, in that many self-assessment taxpayers will be subject to taxes in more than one jurisdiction.

Enforcement

A tax system is only as good as its enforcement. This means that the penalties for noncompliance and other offenses provided in the law must be applied in practice. If penalties are not properly imposed, public confidence in the tax system will be further eroded. In some cases, tax enforcement relies on the enforcement of laws concerning the underlying tax objects, as with the illegal extraction of groundwater (described earlier), minerals, and timber to avoid the loss of associated tax revenues.

Beyond lost tax revenue, a further consequence of the failure to intensify enforcement of local government tax laws and regulations is economic distortion, as businesses gravitate to regions with weak enforcement, where they can benefit from lower taxes, which will give them a competitive advantage over businesses domiciled where tax enforcement is strict.

Taxpayers need to know that noncompliance will have consequences if they are to have an incentive to comply with their tax obligations. Moreover, even if tax delinquents face potential penalties, they will have little incentive to comply if they know that the penalties are unlikely to materialize if they can induce LTA officers to look the other way or reduce the assessments. The actual application of legislated penalties is, thus, a prerequisite for improved taxpayer compliance.

Enforcement standards across all local governments need to be raised. The Performance Indicator Standard for Local Tax Administration (SIKAP) diagnostic tool can improve LTA enforcement if its enforcement performance measures are adopted and disseminated, and if individual LTA enforcement achievements are published annually.

TRAMPIL Website

As a first step toward sustaining the impetus of its tax administration improvements, TRAMPIL developed a website for disseminating knowledge products to local governments on local-source revenue mobilization, and supported its implementation by the Directorate General of Fiscal Balance (DGFB). The website was intended to improve local government taxation through a framework that TRAMPIL designed, initiated, and supported. It was recommended that it be hosted on the Ministry of Finance (MOF) server and administered by the DGFB. Its product menu included the TRAMPIL outputs described in the "Success Achieved by TRAMPIL in Pilot Local Governments" section. Local governments can choose products off the shelf and apply them as deemed most appropriate for their particular circumstances.

While the TRAMPIL website initiative was an excellent starting point and an efficient channel for disseminating tax reform methodologies to all local governments across Indonesia, it alone was insufficient to ensure the sustainability of local government tax reforms undertaken to date. It was one thing to make transformation information available to local governments, but quite another to get them to access and apply it.

Therefore, local governments will need incentives to choose the TRAMPIL website products on offer, as well as incentives to embark on reform in the first place.[60] They will undoubtedly need advice and training on how to use the products they select, which will require the development of additional products that can be uploaded to the website to enable further dissemination.

It is recommended that the DGFB be the institution that directs knowledge sharing to local governments and to maintain and fund knowledge dissemination. Other knowledge products specific to particular local governments could be distributed hierarchically, with the DGFB disseminating them to provinces, which would disseminate them, in turn, to their districts and cities. Provincial governments should assume the responsibility for facilitating the sharing of good practices with their districts and cities, troubleshooting for them, and for coordinating their reform programs.

In addition, a bottom–up knowledge-sharing mechanism should operate concurrently with this top–down dissemination. Local government experience would inform the appropriate solutions for tax reform, from which other local governments could benefit.

Overall Improvement

The four pilot local governments substantially improved the collections of local-source revenues from 2015 and 2018, as shown in Table 4.

Table 4: Pilot Local Government Local-Source Tax Revenue, 2015 and 2018

Pilot Local Government	2015 (Rp)	2018 (Rp)	Increase (%)
Badung			
PBB-P2	190,639,141,226	205,568,318,326	7.8
BPHTB	264,286,116,921	498,174,419,219	88.5
Hotel tax	1,589,717,486,481	2,236,311,260,005	40.0
Restaurant tax	331,409,055,715	624,456,631,010	88.0
Parking service tax	13,571,925,663	24,704,858,685	82.0
Entertainment tax	40,272,237,871	80,288,902,447	99.4
Advertising tax	3,138,459,857	2,339,863,129	(25.4)
Street lighting tax	119,767,754,088	137,523,792,755	14.8
Groundwater tax	54,650,237,871	63,502,870,562	16.0
Nonmetallic minerals tax	56,103,750	40,867,000	(27.2)
Swallows' nest tax	0	0	...
Total	**2,607,408,519,443**	**3,872,911,883,138**	**48.5**

continued on next page

---

60 Incentivization is discussed in Chapter 4.

Table 4: *Continued*

	2015	2018	% Increase
Balikpapan			
PBB-P2	79,066,865,000	90,186,192,508	14.1
BPHTB	82,787,710,000	85,591,587,053	3.4
Hotel tax	37,490,029,000	44,215,141,346	17.9
Restaurant tax	57,868,950,000	83,249,949,477	43.9
Parking service tax	11,668,390,000	19,930,159,455	70.8
Entertainment tax	16,871,732,000	24,237,334,052	43.7
Advertising tax	7,920,666,000	9,223,028,948	16.4
Street lighting tax	89,296,856,000	114,417,353,678	28.1
Groundwater tax	2,021,195,000	2,512,142,076	24.3
Nonmetallic minerals tax	410,367,000	849,201,125	106.9
Swallows' nest tax	43,765,000	29,529,000	48.2
Total	**385,446,525,000**[b]	**474,431,618,718**	**23.1**
Bandung			
PBB-P2	399,912,248,339	552,686,400,078	38.2
BPHTB	399,885,860,295	589,916,701,824	47.5
Hotel tax	215,285,361,236	300,755,546,433	39.7
Restaurant tax	181,868,358,705	325,361,592,033	78.9
Parking service tax	20,234,816,571	43,748,946,680	116.2
Entertainment tax	50,449,101,884	88,856,425,387	76.1
Advertising tax	18,107,052,336	24,255,043,196	34.0
Street lighting tax	178,144,137,262	201,170,794,796	12.9
Groundwater tax	30,260,440,425	33,398,826,889	10.4
Nonmetallic minerals tax	0	0	…
Swallows' nest tax	0	0	…
Total	**1,494,147,377,053**	**2,160,150,277,316**	**44.6**
DKI Jakarta[a]			
PBB-P2	6,807,840,609,166	8,893,076,195,170	30.6
BPHTB	3,609,336,161,480	4,708,906,353,021	30.5
Hotel tax	1,276,285,658,514	1,745,809,882,074	36.8
Restaurant tax	2,290,255,418,530	3,154,969,088,300	37.8
Parking service tax	450,941,851,356	512,750,980,634	13.7

continued on next page

Table 4: *Continued*

	2015	2018	% Increase
Entertainment tax	607,799,682,079	833,684,983,302	37.2
Advertising tax	714,967,327,356	1,014,794,778,877	41.9
Street lighting tax	729,884,587,778	787,107,000,016	7.8
Groundwater tax	105,115,871,134	106,497,711,318	1.3
Nonmetallic minerals tax	0	0	...
Swallows' nest tax	0	0	...
Total	**16,592,427,167,393**	**21,757,596,972,712**	**31.1**

( ) = negative, ... = data not available, BPHTB = duty on the acquisition of land and building rights, DKI = Special Capital Region, PBB-P2 = urban and rural land and building tax, Rp = rupiah.

[a] The DKI Jakarta section of this table contains provisional data.

[b] The values for Balikpapan in 2015, and therefore the total, are rounded off.

Sources: Asian Development Bank, Tax Revenue Administration Modernization and Policy Improvement in Local Governments project; Directorate General of Fiscal Balance (DGFB). 2015. *Realisasi APBD, 2015*. Manila; DGFB. 2018. *Realisasi APBD, 2018*. Manila; Statistics Indonesia.

Across the four pilot local governments, the average overall increase in local-source tax revenue from 2015 to 2018 was just under 37%. Some pilot local governments recorded very substantial improvements in significant contributory taxes, in particular Badung, with its BPHTB and restaurant tax; and Bandung, with restaurant tax.

These increases correlate with the delivery of technical assistance by the TRAMPIL project from its start in early 2015. This does not prove any causal relationship, but it is undeniable that the technical assistance to implement improvements in tax administration methods and processes in the pilot LTAs contributed to higher tax collection.

CHAPTER 4

FURTHER POLICY DEVELOPMENT OPPORTUNITIES

Policy Imperatives

Decentralization is unshakable in Indonesia by virtue of Articles 18, 18A, and 18B of the Constitution; laws derived from them; and simple political reality. The validity of the central government's oversight of local government revenue-raising lies in its constitutional and legal responsibility for national fiscal policy. Within these parameters, the policy imperative is to find new sources of local-source revenue that conform with central government policy. While proposed amendments to Law 28/2009 would broaden the taxing capacity of local governments, a number of tax policy issues still demand rigorous analysis. This chapter addresses some areas requiring further effort. The priority is on policies that could increase local-source tax revenue by expanding the existing tax base, not by simply increasing rates.

Application of Existing Taxes

Despite the call for more local-source revenue, most local governments taxed, at least nominally, most of the tax bases permitted under Law 28/2009. Figure 13 shows that 360 of 501 districts and cities (including DKI Jakarta)—or 71.9%—applied at least nine of the local taxes available to them in 2018.[61] This means that increases in local-source revenue would have to come from the following:

(i)   immediate improvements in tax administration;

(ii)   higher maximum tax rates and a limited broadening of the tax base in the short to medium term, as envisaged by proposed amendments to Law 28/2009; and

(iii)   a much-expanded tax base in the long term.

Notwithstanding the possibilities of local-source revenue generation that Law 28/2009 offers, some local governments have been slow to respond fully to the central government's surrender of some of its tax collection authority. Of the 28.1% of the 501 districts and cities that did not apply all the local taxes available to them, 56, or 11.2%, applied seven or fewer. The reasons for this should be investigated. If no convincing reason can be found, the question is this: Why is the rest of the country subsidizing through proportionately greater central government transfers local governments that leave unraised much of their available local-source revenue? Assuming that there is no compelling reason why any of these 56 local governments are not using all their powers of taxation, the prospects for their collecting more local-source tax are much greater in the short term because they can simply tap more widely into their existing tax base under Law 28/2009, and improve their administrative efficiency.

While most local governments apply most of the taxes available to them, a closer examination reveals that a significant portion of them fail to tax particular objects. As seen in Chapter 3, property taxes are important generators of tax revenue for local governments. While the urban and rural land and building tax (PBB-P2) is imposed by 98.0% of local governments, and the duty on the acquisition of land and building rights (BPHTB) by 96.6%, they are not necessarily the most frequently imposed taxes across all the districts and cities.

---

[61]   Many of those that applied only 9 or 10 of the 11 taxes available were unable to apply more because some tax bases, such as those for swallows' nests and nonmetallic minerals and rocks, are not present in their regions.

Figure 13: Number of Taxes Applied by Districts and Cities, 2018

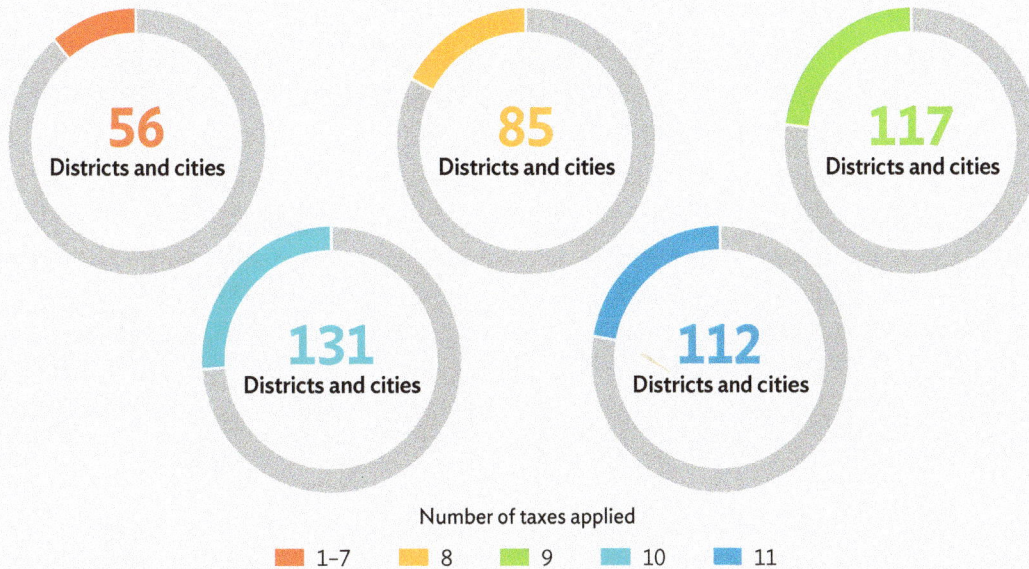

56
Districts and cities

85
Districts and cities

117
Districts and cities

131
Districts and cities

112
Districts and cities

Number of taxes applied

■ 1–7 ■ 8 ■ 9 ■ 10 ■ 11

Source: Asian Development Bank, Tax Revenue Administration Modernization and Policy Improvement in Local Governments project.

Figure 14: Percentages of Districts and Cities Not Imposing Particular Taxes, 2018

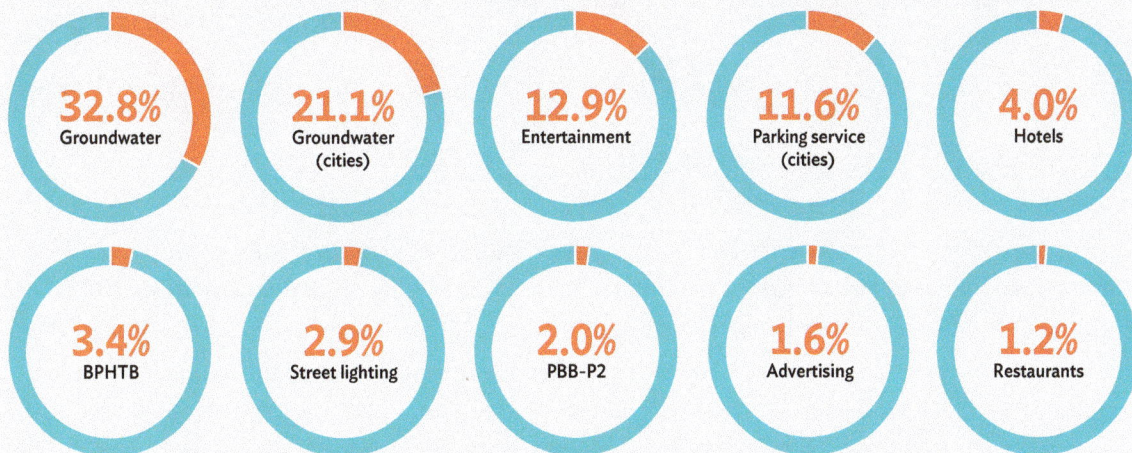

32.8%
Groundwater

21.1%
Groundwater
(cities)

12.9%
Entertainment

11.6%
Parking service
(cities)

4.0%
Hotels

3.4%
BPHTB

2.9%
Street lighting

2.0%
PBB-P2

1.6%
Advertising

1.2%
Restaurants

BPHTB = duty on the acquisition of land and building rights, PBB-P2 = urban and rural land and building tax.
Note: The Special Capital Region of Jakarta is the only provincial-level government included in these calculations.
Source: ADB estimates.

As shown in Figure 14, the percentage of local governments that imposed the restaurant tax in 2018 was 98.8%; advertising tax, 98.4%; street lighting tax, 97.8%; and the hotel tax, 96.2%. Increasing the use of these local-source taxes, together with property taxes, would improve administrative competence and boost tax revenues. Going beyond that, however, will require new and innovative policy design.

However, at the other end of the spectrum, there appears to be a greater scope for local revenue mobilization through the groundwater tax, which is unused by one-third of all nonprovincial local governments. That 21.1% of all cities do not tax groundwater is telling, as demand for groundwater is high in cities, and would therefore seem to offer considerable potential tax revenue. However, as noted in Chapter 3, the ability of this tax to produce more revenue depends, maybe to a considerable extent, on the ability of local governments to police illegal water extraction.

It is also surprising that just under 12% of cities did not tax parking services in 2018. Given the seemingly unending growth in urban traffic volume and congestion, the environmental impact, and the need for continual investment in roads, parking service taxes offer a potentially lucrative way to generate additional revenue while mitigating through deterrence the harm done by excessive driving in cities. However, a wider application of the parking service tax must go beyond shopping malls. A level playing field would require a broadening of the application of the tax to take in parking charges levied by the local governments themselves for the use of their public parking lots.

A push for greater local-source revenue would, however, open up greater opportunities for corruption than currently exists with the transfer of funds from the central government to the local governments. As one observer puts it, "Decentralization has created new oligarchs at the local levels. Corruption, collusion, and nepotism are now widespread in local governments."[62] Therefore, it follows that if corruption is to be viewed as something worse than just another cost of doing business, it must be confronted in tandem with any further devolution of revenue-raising powers to the local governments. This is another argument for the holistic approach to governance discussed in Chapter 3. To be sustainable, any additional devolution of tax authority must be implemented with an eye to the barriers to its eventual success, and these barriers must be tackled simultaneously.

Reliable and Timely Reporting of Data

The quality of policy decisions depends on the accuracy of the data on which they are based. The Directorate General of Fiscal Balance (DGFB) as the repository of local government revenue data is not complete, properly detailed, nor collated on a timely basis. For example, when viewed on 1 October 2019, realized tax collections by tax type across all provincial, district, and city governments in 2017 were still incomplete; and apparently finalized data, where provided, were often presented in rounded numbers, typically to the nearest trillion rupiah. Further, on the same date, the records of realized tax collections by tax type in 2016 were incomplete for almost half of the country's 528 local governments of all types, nearly 3 years after the end of that year.

Moreover, DGFB regional revenue realization data are incompatible with Statistics Indonesia data. For example, on 1 October 2019, the DGFB publication *Realisasi Anggaran Pendapatan dan Belanja Daerah 2017 (Realization of the Regional Revenue and Expenditure Budget 2017)* disclosed that the hotel tax

---

62   Footnote 20, p. 3.

collected by Badung district in 2017 amounted to Rp1,061,897,543,152, while Statistics Indonesia listed it as Rp2,030,000,000,000, almost twice as much. It is unclear whether this discrepancy was because of incomplete or estimated data, or for some other reason. Whatever the explanation, the magnitude of the discrepancy makes data from either source a shaky basis on which to make policy decisions.

The dangers of devising policy on the basis of data that are out of date or otherwise faulty are obvious. A glaring case in point is again from Badung district, on Indonesia's tourist magnet that is Bali: as of 11 December 2019, there were still no data on hotel tax collections in the DGFB publication *Realisasi Anggaran Pendapatan dan Belanja Daerah 2016 (Realization of the Regional Revenue and Expenditure Budget 2016)*. If the DGFB or the local government wished to reconsider its policies concerning hotel tax targets or rates, it could result in little confidence in using this database.

Weak data gathering and reporting are further reasons for local governments to use a proper information and communication technology (ICT) system that records receipts of each revenue type in each local government on a regular basis, preferably in real time or at least daily. With such a system, the reporting of tax collections by tax type to central government agencies could be done in a matter of days, rather than months or years, even if the ICT system is not uniform across all local governments.

Greater discipline and consistency must be imposed to ensure the accurate recording and submission of local government revenue data. This may require central government regulations that specify minimum data-recording standards, uniform reporting formats, time limits for data submission, and penalties for failure to comply. Such regulations would also need to apply to the provinces, which act as intermediary data repositories between district and city governments, on the one hand, and the central government, on the other. As explained in Chapter 3, a greater degree of homogeneity across the local governments' administrative procedural systems would alleviate current data reporting shortcomings. Therefore, it would make sense to [verify] whether deficiencies in data reporting are adequately resolved by the adoption—as expounded in Government Regulation No. 12 of 2019 on regional financial management— of the harmonized standard chart of accounts for financial and statistical reporting.

Alignment with Central Government Policy

As discussed earlier, local government tax policies must conform to the central government's macroeconomic policies to encourage investment and economic growth. In accordance with requirements, the Capital Investment Coordinating Board, a ministerial body reporting directly to the President, is charged with implementing policy and service coordination to boost domestic and foreign direct investment by creating a conducive investment climate through incentives and regulatory reform, including faster licensing.[63] Local government tax policies must integrate with those initiatives.

---

[63]   A presidential instruction issued on 22 November 2019 (Inpres No. 7 of 2019 on the acceleration of ease of doing business) gave the head of the Capital Investment Coordinating Board a full mandate to issue all business licenses formerly administered by government ministries and other government institutions.

Moreover, a sustainable tax system does not undermine economic efficiency by impeding or reducing the productive capacity. A 50% reduction in the maximum rate of taxation applicable to the acquisition of rights to land and/or buildings, stipulated in Article 28(1)(a) of the proposed amendments to Law 28/2009, is an example of a tax that is compatible with this objective in that it lowers a hurdle inhibiting the most efficient allocation of resources.

Areas That Warrant Further Policy Analysis

The tax policy support under the TRAMPIL project identified a number of areas that invited further policy analysis and recommendations. This chapter presents nine of them for consideration by policy makers. They include the benefit principle, the cascading effect of local taxes on goods and services, exemptions from the PBB-P2, transfer taxes, piggybacking on national taxes, the tourist accommodation tax, behavioral taxes (cigarette excise, sugar and fat, and environmental taxes), betterment taxes and local franchise fees, and user charges.

Benefit Principle

A fundamental tenet underlying the imposition of taxation is the benefit principle. At its simplest, it dictates a tax burden on citizens or entities congruent with the benefits that they receive. Ensuring that a tax is fair, and linking it to the local services that it is intended to fund, improves taxpayer acceptance. In short, a local government financial system will run better if local taxes and the benefits of local government expenditure are closely correlated.

User charges ensure that an entity that obtains the exclusive use of goods or services provided by a local government pays for that benefit, in the same way entities pay for privately provided goods and services. Where exclusive use is not possible, general benefit taxes are imposed on the group of people who benefit jointly from the goods or services, such as taxes levied on motor vehicles and fuels, the revenues from which can be used to construct and maintain roads, which benefit road users as a class. Benefit-related taxes send the right signals to local governments to fund the optimal supply of public goods and services that are subject to taxes.

Adherence to the benefit principle improves accountability and thereby puts a check on local government decision makers. If a local government spends too little on the benefits that the tax is supposed to fund, the local community, which pays for them through taxes or fees, can respond directly to the local government with submissions and protests or, ultimately, vote the government out of office. For example, a local government's thirst for revenue may induce excessive taxation of a particular sector without the provision of commensurate benefits to it. This has occurred in Indonesia when, for instance, several local governments set street lighting tax rates at the maximum stipulated in Law 28/2009 to increase their revenues, but without any accompanying increase in the provision of street lighting, as required by Article 56(3) of Law 28/2009.

However, such accountability is not foolproof, so behavioral constraints on local governments need to be imposed within a central government framework. Although a tax may benefit the majority of a local community, its imposition on a particular sector, especially when excessive, may contravene central government macroeconomic policies. For example, excessive local government taxation of commerce may thwart investment in local businesses, contravening the central government's policies and incentives designed to encourage investment, though it may substantially increase the local government's income while relieving the tax burden on most local residents.

Another political accountability problem is that taxpayers hold the government agency that collected their taxes accountable for the benefits they have received or failed to receive. However, the provider of the benefits may not necessarily be the same government that collected the taxes in the first place. So, when challenged about the quantity and/or quality of benefits, the government agency in charge of providing the benefits in question can simply deflect the blame to the government entity that initially imposed that tax for its failure to pass on all that funds it had collected.

Such are the potential problems of imposing motor vehicle taxes in Indonesia. A mismatch exists between the imposition and collection of motor vehicle taxes by the provincial governments and the expenditures by the districts and cities on benefits for road users, notably road maintenance and expansion. Excluding DKI Jakarta, provincial taxes in 2017 comprised just under 63% of all local tax revenue, of which just under 85% consisted of motor vehicle taxes. The provincial governments retain 70% of motor vehicle tax revenue (including revenue from the tax on the transfer of ownership of motor vehicles) and 30% of motor vehicle fuel tax revenue, but the districts and cities pay for the bulk of local government expenditure on roads. Moreover, districts and cities have no directly corresponding revenue-gathering mechanism, other than the relatively insignificant parking services tax, for tapping the car owners who are the beneficiaries of these public goods.

In summary, applying the benefit principle requires a correspondence between the government body that collects the tax revenue and the government body that pays for the benefits to taxpayers. Otherwise, taxpayers may receive only scant benefits for the amount of taxes they paid because the government body that had collected the taxes retained some or all of the revenue, instead of allocating sufficient funding to the provider of government benefits. Thus, policy makers should assess how well the current tax system applies the benefit principle.

It should be noted that, in addition to the benefit principle, other criteria determine which taxes are appropriately levied by local governments, as follows:

(i)   The tax base is immobile, for instance when the tax object is physically immovable or fixed within the local government jurisdiction, making the tax difficult to evade.

(ii) The tax base is distributed relatively evenly among regions.

(iii) The tax is not distortionary, having a neutral effect on the behavior of taxpayers and, in particular, having no negative effect on regional economic growth.

(iv) The tax provides stable revenue flows to local governments.

Tax policy must trade the benefits of some of these principles against other benefits. For example, taxes on the transfer of property—either motor vehicles, or land and buildings—broadly meet the criterion of stable revenue flows, but do not satisfy the criterion of avoiding distortionary taxes. That such taxes are widely imposed by local governments in Indonesia is a testament to decision makers' preference for ensuring stable tax flows. Therefore,

> "[d]esigning appropriate policies and prioritizing among them requires reference to values to determine what is the appropriate trade-off between different goals and taking into account the political and social consequences of implementing them."[64]

By contrast, annual taxes on land and building ownership comfortably fit all the criteria above, which is why property taxes are typically levied by local governments, in Indonesia and internationally. As seen in Chapter 3, though, a tremendous scope exists for improving local governments' administration of them.

To apply the criteria rationally to local government decision-making would require a cost–benefit analysis of each application. This requirement would invite further external technical assistance for most local governments.

Cascading Effect of Local Taxes on Goods and Services

Under Law 28/2009, as it currently stands, local taxes on goods and services, which are effectively sales taxes, are imposed mostly on final consumption. To the extent that they are levied on goods and services that are resold or used commercially, they have a cascading effect, as they are built into the costs of goods and services, upon which further tax may by imposed later, in effect creating a tax on a tax.

Proposed amendments to Law 28/2009 aggravate the cascading effect by accumulating taxes at each stage of a supply chain. In particular, articles 45(1), 46(2)(b), and 46(4) of the proposed amendments contemplate the imposition of taxes on motor fuel and electricity at each stage of the supply chain, by stating the following:

(i)   The subjects of the tax on the use of motor vehicle fuel are consumers of motor vehicle fuel (Article 45[1]).

(ii) The payer of taxes on the use of motor vehicle fuel or electricity is an individual or an entity providing fuel for motor vehicles or providing electricity (Article 46[2][b]).

(iii) Providers of motor vehicle fuel, as referred to in Article 46(2)(b), include producers and/or importers of motor vehicle fuel, both for sale and for their own use (Article 46[4]).

These provisions cause a cascade of accumulating local sales taxes on production or importation, wholesale, and retail—the whole supply chain. This is economically inefficient because it pushes up the cost structure of the economy. Although multiple cascades of local taxes are particularly germane to the supply and

---

[64]   S. G. Reddy. 2019. Economics' Biggest Success Story Is a Cautionary Tale. *Foreign Policy*. 22 October. https://foreignpolicy. com/2019/10/22/economics-development-rcts-esther-duflo-abhijit-banerjee-michael-kremer-nobel/.

distribution of motor fuel and electricity, they easily amount to a double taxation on the supply of other taxable goods and services to businesses. The cascading effect is illustrated in Table 5, using the example of a fuel supply chain.

Table 5 presents four scenarios in which fuel is imported for Rp100 million: two-stage and three-stage supply chains, each with and without the cascading effect of multiple-level taxation. In a three-stage supply chain, the importer sells the imported fuel to a fuel distributor, who then sells it on to a fuel retailer, who finally sells it to the end consumer. In the two-stage supply chain, the importer sells directly to the retailer, who then sells it to the end consumer. Under all four scenarios, the profit margin for the supplier is 5% of the price paid, and at each stage of the supply chain, there is a provincial government tax set at the maximum rate of 10%. In the three-stage supply chain with the cascading effect, the result of the multiple-level tax is an increase in the fuel price of 21% for the end consumer, in this case from Rp127.34 million to Rp154.09 million. In the two-stage supply chain with the cascading effect, the tax raises the price of the fuel by 10% for the end consumer, from Rp121.28 million to Rp133.41 million.

Table 5: Cascading Effect of Local Taxation on a Fuel Supply Chain (Rp million)

Supply Chain Role	Three-Stage Supply Chain		Two-Stage Supply Chain	
	With Cascading Effect	Without Cascading Effect	With Cascading Effect	Without Cascading Effect
Importer				
Cost price of fuel	100.00	100.00	100.00	100.00
Profit margin (5%)	5.00	5.00	5.00	5.00
Subtotal	105.00	105.00	105.00	105.00
Tax (10%)	10.50	0.00	10.50	0.00
Selling price	115.50	105.00	115.50	105.00
Distributor				
Cost price of fuel	115.50	105.00		
Profit margin (5%)	5.78	5.25		
Subtotal	121.28	110.25		
Tax (10%)	12.13	0.00		
Selling price to retailer	133.41	110.25		
Retailer				
Cost price of fuel	133.40	110.25	115.50	105.00
Profit margin (5%)	6.67	5.51	5.78	5.25
Subtotal	140.08	115.76	121.28	110.25
Tax (10%)	14.01	11.58	12.13	11.03
Selling price to end consumer	154.09	127.34	133.41	121.28

Rp = rupiah.

Notes: 1. The value-added tax is ignored in this example because its impact is assumed to be neutral here, with no effect on the outcome.

2. An empty cell means that the column head does not apply. A two-stage supply chain does not include a distributor.

Source: Asian Development Bank, Tax Revenue Administration Modernization and Policy Improvement in Local Governments project.

For a tax to be truly a consumption tax, it should be imposed only at the point of final sale—in the case of motor vehicle fuel, at the gas station where the fuel is sold for private use. In practical terms, this can be achieved only by (i) allowing commercial purchasers a tax refund, or (ii) exempting commercial purchasers at the point of sale. Both approaches inevitably increase the costs of taxpayer compliance enforcement and tax administration.

To the extent that the cascading effect applies to motor fuel taxes, it serves as an environmental tax because the accumulating price hikes dampen consumer demand for the fuel, thus, benefiting the environment. However, tax policy makers must weigh the environmental benefit against the increase in the general business cost structure arising from the cascading affect, with its ramifications for business and investment in Indonesia. This is a further example of a trade-off of conflicting objectives for tax policy.

One remedy to the broader problem of cascading local government taxes is to remove the local government taxation of goods and services altogether, in favor of a national value-added tax. This approach is discussed in the "Piggybacking on National Taxes" section.

Exemptions from the Urban and Rural Land and Building Tax

Article 77(4) of Law 28/2009 sets the minimum sale value for the PBB-P2 at Rp10 million. To protect poor households from the tax, local governments must allow an exemption from the PBB-P2 of at least Rp10 million. Box 8 illustrates how DKI Jakarta has gone further by setting its exemption at Rp1 billion and fully exempting "meritorious taxpayers," a category that includes veterans, retired police, military personnel, civil servants, national heroes, honorary medal recipients, and former presidents and vice-presidents. A policy question is whether these total exemptions from the PBB-P2 are the most appropriate way to recognize the services of meritorious taxpayers, in light of the generally accepted criteria for taxes discussed above.

Other options for exemptions for poorer local residents include allowing older low-income property owners who are asset-rich, but income-poor, to defer payment of the PBB-P2 until their property is sold or inherited, or giving graduated tax rebates to low-income taxpayers.[65]

Whenever tax exemptions are granted, however, the inevitable question is: Who will bear the cost? Local government revenue lost to exemptions must be found elsewhere or cut from government expenditure altogether.[66] To conform with the central government's investment and economic growth policies, local governments would need to restrict the impact on businesses of additional tax measures to compensate for the exemptions. Again, the trade-off between revenue enhancement, equity, and broader economic imperatives must be evaluated in order to identify the optimal extent of exemptions.

---

[65]   H. Blöchliger. 2015. Reforming the Tax on Immovable Property: Taking Care of the Unloved. *OECD Economics Department Working Papers.* No. 1205. Paris: OECD. pp. 22–23. https://www.oecd-ilibrary.org/docserver/5js30tw0n7kg-en.pdf?expires= 1618885139&id=id&accname=guest&checksum=1E9CAA55EE2C8F1D9D11707E2E9248F8; Government of New Zealand, New Zealand Productivity Commission. 2019. *Local Government Funding and Financing—Draft Report.* Wellington, New Zealand. pp. 202–206. https://www.productivity.govt.nz/assets/Documents/faacf52aab/ProdCom_Draft-report_Local-government-funding-and-financing.pdf.

[66]   When government expenditure is reduced to compensate for revenue lost due to tax exemptions, the cost is borne by those who no longer benefit from the forgone expenditure.

Box 8: Jakarta Working on New Tax Policies

"The [Jakarta] city administration has issued Gubernatorial Regulation No. 38/2019 on PBB-P2 exemptions for individuals or institutions whose land and building assets amounted to less than Rp1 billion ($70,175) in taxable value of property (NJOP).

"Article 2A stipulates PBB-P2 tax exemptions on land and building ownership and on transfers of land ownership.

"As stipulated in Article 4A, that tax policy only applies until Dec. 31 this year...

"Despite the expiration date, [DKI Jakarta Governor] Anies emphasized that the administration had no intention to end the policy.

"On the contrary, he said the administration was currently drafting a policy to expand the scope of PBB-P2 tax exemptions, which initially applied to tax objects worth less than Rp1 billion, to meritorious taxpayers, including veterans, retired police and military personnel, retired civil servants, national heroes, honorary medal recipients, and former presidents and vice-presidents, with certain requirements...

"The new policy was likely to reduce the city's tax revenue, Anies admitted, but he said the administration could potentially earn more once the fiscal cadastre was completed...

"One of the attempts to increase tax revenue is the recently issued Gubernatorial Regulation No. 41/2019 on PBB-P2. Article 3 of that regulation stipulates that taxpayers who own unused land in premium areas like Jl. MH Thamrin, Jl. Sudirman, Jl. Rasuna Said, Jl. Gatot Subroto and Jl. MT Haryono are required to pay a double tax rate.

"However, Article 3 section 4 stipulates that those who transform the unused land into open green space are required to pay only half the general tax rate...

"Moreover, Anies claimed the administration was preparing a special regulation for houses in upscale areas.

"City councillor Santoso from the Democratic Party, who heads Commission C overseeing finance... hoped the PBB-P2 tax exemption for meritorious people should be strictly defined, because some of them could be categorized as 'fortunate people.'

"'[The city administration] needs to consider [their economic] standing,' he said.

"...Rusli Abdullah, researcher at the Institute for Development of Economics and Finance (INDEF)... said... the expanded PBB-P2 tax exemption... could be deemed discriminating, as many residents were unable to earn a proper living. He urged the administration to maximize efforts against tax evasion.

"Center for Indonesia Taxation Analysis (CITA) executive director Yustinus Prastowo said the administration's taxation policies had to protect lower-middle income earners, while tax collection from commercial entities should be 'optimized.'"

DKI = Special Capital Region, PBB-P2 = urban and rural land and building tax.
Source: S. Atika. 2019. Jakarta Working on New Tax Policies. *The Jakarta Post.* 24 April.

The Rp10 million minimum exemption is available to all PBB-P2 taxpayers, not just the poorer ones it is intended to protect. Denying the exemption to wealthy property owners without causing distortion is not as straightforward as simply disallowing taxpayers whose property holdings in the aggregate exceed the threshold. Doing so would impose an undesirable marginal tax on taxpayers whose property value slightly exceeded the threshold. The prospect of a sharp increase in a taxpayer's PBB-P2 liability from zero to the full amount when a property appreciates to just above the exemption threshold encourages taxpayers to find ways to avoid complying with their tax obligations.

A better and generally politically more acceptable way to deny the concession to taxpayers who do not need it is to abate the exemption depending on how much the tax object sales value (NJOP) of the property exceeds the threshold. Wealthy property owners do not get the exemption because the aggregate value of their properties will far exceed the threshold. Box 9 illustrates how exemption abatement works.

Box 9: Example of an Abatement of the Urban and Rural Land and Building Tax Exemption

Assume that

(i)   A local government allows taxpayers a PBB-P2 exemption for the first Rp1 billion of their aggregate NJOPs,

(ii)   The PBB-P2 rate is 0.3% of the NJOP,

(iii)   Taxpayer A owns one property with an NJOP of Rp1.2 billion, and

(iv)   Taxpayer B owns many properties with an aggregate NJOP value of Rp20 billion.

Taxpayer A must pay a PBB-P2 of Rp600,000, or 0.3% x (Rp1,200,000,000 – 1,000,000,000); and Taxpayer B must pay a PBB-P2 of Rp57,000,000, or 0.3% x (20,000,000,000 – 1,000,000,000). Taxpayer A faces an effective PBB-P2 tax rate of 0.05%, or (600,000/1,200,000,000) x 100, which is far lower than that faced by Taxpayer B, whose effective PBB-P2 tax rate is 0.285%, or (57,000,000/20,000,000,000) x 100. The much wealthier Taxpayer B gets the benefit of the Rp1 billion exemption, which saves both taxpayers Rp3 million, though Taxpayer B's wealth suggests that she does not really need it.

If the exemption were simply removed for taxpayers whose NJOPs exceed Rp1 billion, both taxpayers would have an additional Rp3 million each to pay in PBB-P2, which would be an increase of 500% for Taxpayer A and a 5.26% increase for Taxpayer B. Both taxpayers would then pay an effective tax rate equal to the nominal rate of 0.3%. Although this approach preserves the exemption for property owners whose aggregate NJOPs do not exceed Rp1 billion, the outcome for Taxpayer A is clearly inequitable, as the marginal tax rate increase that he would pay with the removal of the exemption would raise his effective rate sixfold because his NJOP is marginally above the exemption threshold. Also, despite the large wealth disparity between Taxpayer A and Taxpayer B, they both pay the same effective tax rate.

To mitigate this inequitable outcome, now assume that the exemption abates by Rp1 for each rupiah that exceeds the exemption threshold. This means that, if the NJOP is Rp1 above the exemption amount, or Rp1,000,000,001, the exemption falls by Rp1, to Rp999,999,999. If the NJOP is Rp2 above the exemption amount, or Rp1,000,000,002, the exemption falls by Rp2 to Rp999,999,998. The exemption is finally eliminated at an NJOP of Rp2 billion.

Adopting this methodology, Taxpayer A would now pay a PBB-P2 of Rp1,200,000, or 0.3% x (1,200,000,000 – [1,000,000,000 – 200,000,000]). Taxpayer A's effective tax rate is now 0.1% (1,200,000/1,200,000,000) x 100. Taxpayer B must now pay PBB-P2 of Rp60,000,000, or 0.3% x (20,000,000,000 – [1,000,000,000 – 1,000,000,000]). Taxpayer B's effective tax rate is now equal to the nominal rate of 0.3%, (60,000,000/20,000,000,000) x 100. Taxpayer A still gets some benefit from the exemption, though it progressively phases out as his NJOP approaches Rp2 billion. The richer Taxpayer B now gets no benefit from the Rp1 billion exemption because it is no longer available to taxpayers whose NJOPs exceed Rp2 billion. This is a far more equitable outcome from Taxpayer A's perspective and is a far more equitable outcome from the local community's perspective with respect to the treatment of Taxpayer B.

Further, the local government collects an additional Rp3,600,000 in PBB-P2: Rp600,000 more from Taxpayer A and Rp3,000,000 more from Taxpayer B.

NJOP = tax object sales value, PBB-P2 = urban and rural land and building tax, Rp = rupiah.

Source: Asian Development Bank, Tax Revenue Administration Modernization and Policy Improvement in Local Governments project.

While the example in Box 9 adopts a simple rupiah-for-rupiah trade-off between the amount of NJOP above the exemption threshold and the amount by which the threshold is reduced, the rate of abatement is ultimately a political decision. Phasing out an exemption means less revenue for the local government from some taxpayers, but it has no effect on tax revenue from taxpayers whose NJOPs exceed the abatement limit, compared with the simple abolition of the exemption once the threshold is met. The ultimate revenue effect depends on the composition of property owners and the aggregate value of their NJOPs. Analysis of those two variables will inform the selection of an appropriate abatement rate. The exemption abatement mechanism described above has the advantage of preserving the full exemption for NJOPs below the threshold and easing the burden on taxpayers who are just above the threshold, while not extending the exemption to taxpayers who do not need it.

Transfer Taxes

Transfer taxes are distortionary, creating economic inefficiencies because they deter asset upgrading by owners that are subject to them. Transfer taxes encourage tax evasion because they incentivize the undervaluation of asset values, and thus generate inaccurate fiscal cadastre values for land and buildings, which undermine the veracity of PBB-P2 assessments.

Though property and motor vehicle transfer taxes are easy to administer, consideration should be given to making them gradually less important in the matrix of local government taxes.

Article 87(5) of Law 28/2009 addresses the taxation of transfers of land and buildings. It allows a tax exemption of at least Rp300 million when the property is directly transferred to direct relatives through an inheritance.[67] While that concession mitigates the economic inefficiency of the tax, it can also have the opposite effect, providing an incentive for the owner to hold the property while still alive. Moreover, the ability of local governments to offer such an exemption should be examined on tax equity grounds, as it facilitates the accumulation of untaxed wealth. Such exemptions also provide opportunities for tax avoidance—and therefore create market distortions and tax competition between regions—by inducing property owners later in life to reside or acquire properties in regions where the concession is offered, depending on whether it is granted to the tax subject or the tax object.

Piggybacking on National Taxes

Central government tax collection and the allocation of collected taxes to local governments is an attractive way to fund local governments from the perspective of administrative efficiency. It avoids the duplication of tax assessment and collection, and as a result conserves resources. However, this sharing system conflicts with the central government's decentralization policy, which requires local governments to progressively generate more of their own funds to finance their expenditures. This direction is reinforced by the current debate over the allocation formulas in Law 33/2004.

---

[67] In addition to this provision, Article 87(4) provides for a general exemption of Rp60 million per tax subject.

However, an immediate factor that restricts local-source revenue mobilization is the low economic activity in many regions—too low to generate sufficient local-source revenue to fund their expenditure requirements. This means that, at least in the short to medium term, those regions must continue to rely on central government allocations. On the assumption that these allocations will continue, the proposed amendments to Law 33/2004 are intended to iron out inconsistencies in the allocation formulas.

Direct revenue sharing between the central and local governments occurs mostly with the personal income tax (PIT) and the land and building tax for mining, forestry, and plantations (PBB-P3). These taxes are collected by the Directorate General of Taxation (DGT) and then shared on a derivation basis with the local governments. This revenue-sharing mechanism is different from the imposition of *opsen* (surtaxes) on tax objects. The surtax approach, which is advocated in the proposed amendments to Law 28/2009, is often viewed as the local governments piggybacking on the central government tax revenue, implying that the local governments are getting a free ride.

One disadvantage of local government reliance on surtaxes and allocations from the central government, especially when the allocations from central government tax are by derivation, is the local governments' inability to police the collection of underlying taxes within their own jurisdictions. If limited DGT resources require an emphasis on the collection of taxes on which the surcharge is not levied or that are not otherwise allocated to local governments, such as the corporate income tax, there is little that the local governments can do to increase the collection of the underlying tax. To the extent that the DGT fails to collect the full amount of taxes in a locality, the local government will suffer along with the central government. A better alternative to relying on central government tax surcharges is to explore the ways in which local tax authorities can become involved in the wider application and collection of those taxes, as in the joint audit arrangements discussed in Chapter 3.

The central government's current sharing of PIT revenue originated in a 2008 amendment to Law 7/1983 on income tax, through Article 31C of Law 36/2008, which took effect on 1 January 2009.[68] Article 31C requires that "[t]ax revenue collected from individual resident taxpayers and income tax of Article 21 [of Law 36/2008] withheld by the employer, shall be shared with the share of 80% for the central government and 20% for local government where the taxpayer is registered."[69] The fundamental problem with this law is that Indonesia has a large informal sector, low income-tax compliance, and a high exemption threshold, which makes PIT a weak base for revenue sharing and for the imposition of surcharges. These and other policy shortcomings of using the PIT base as a source of local government revenue are analyzed in detail in Appendix 3.

---

[68]   According to Hofman and Kaiser, "the sharing of the personal income tax on a derivation basis was decided at the last moment, and inspired by a conversation the Minister of Finance had on a trip to disseminate the decentralization laws" (footnote 17).

[69]   Article 21 requires employers to withhold income tax from taxable salaries and other compensation payable to their employees.

Tourist Accommodation Tax

Two fundamental tax-related issues need to be addressed in the tourism industry. These are (i) policy regarding the opportunity to broaden local-source tax revenue to meet increased local government expenditure directly attributable to tourism; and (ii) how administrators can counter noncompliance with the hotel tax, including in the use of online booking platforms.[70]

Following contemporary international developments, a new potential source of local government revenue is the tourist accommodation tax, which has been adopted abroad, notably in Amsterdam; Tokyo; and Queenstown, New Zealand. The objective is typically to obtain additional revenue to meet local governments' increased expenditure directly attributable to tourists.

Such a tax, which would extend beyond the current hotel tax, is likely to be lucrative in Indonesia as the country as a whole grows as a tourist destination, and particularly for local governments in regions that attract high numbers of tourists. Due to their greater disposable income and varying preferences, and to the increasing prevalence of tourism taxes internationally, foreign tourists in particular are less likely to object to this tax in Indonesia, especially if it transparently reflects the benefit principle. Indonesia has the additional advantage of being an inexpensive tourist destination.[71] Taking these factors into account, foreigners and Indonesians could pay different tax rates.

The tourist accommodation tax would require robust registration and compliance enforcement to ensure that all suppliers of tourist accommodations are captured. Including those that sell reservations through digital platforms would be particularly pertinent in Indonesia, given the significance of rapidly emerging online reservation services. Tourist accommodation reservations made online in 2017 reached a total of 904,600 through Airbnb alone, an increase of 69% from 2016,[72] earning $84.6 million for Airbnb's 11,200 hosts in Indonesia.[73] However, these accommodation suppliers currently fall outside the tax regime, raising concerns for the Indonesian Hotel and Restaurant Association (Box 10).

---

[70] Also see Chapter 3, in the "Noncompliance" section.

[71] Indonesia ranks sixth internationally for tourism price competitiveness. World Economic Forum. 2019. *The Travel & Tourism Competitiveness Report 2019: Travel and Tourism at a Tipping Point.* Geneva. p. 77. http://www3.weforum.org/docs/WEF_TTCR_2019.pdf.

[72] *The Jakarta Post.* 2018. Indonesian Hosts Welcome over 900,000 Travellers in 2017: Airbnb. 10 January. https://www.thejakartapost.com/travel/2018/01/10/indonesian-hosts-welcome-over-900000-travelers-in-2017-airbnb.html.

[73] Airbnb. 2017. *Airbnb & APEC: Closing Tourism Gaps with Healthy Travel.* San Francisco. p. 28. http://www.asiatraveltips.com/AirbnbAPEC2017Report.pdf.

Box 10: **Hospitality Rules Need Revision: Business Becoming More Costly**

"The Indonesian Hotel and Restaurant Association (PHRI) has called on the government to deregulate the hospitality and tourism industry because existing regulations are no longer compatible with current conditions.

"'Our call for deregulation is to improve competitiveness because existing regulations have made the business costly,' said PHRI deputy chairman Maulana Yusran.

"He added that the hospitality and tourism industry was affected by high licensing fees, taxes, regional levies, water resource taxes and certification costs.

"The industry also faced various other problems including an oversupply of rooms, digital disruption (the appearance of business competitors in the digital era), price wars and certification disputes, Maulana added.

"He said many hoteliers were complaining about Government Regulation No. 55/2016 on regional tax and levy that imposed taxes for complimentary/free of charge services introduced by hotels and restaurants.

"They were also not happy with Law No. 28/2009 on terms and conditions and the procedure in regional tax collection, he added.

"Maulana also pointed out that the types and categorization of hospitality and restaurant businesses should be expanded because [they were] not compatible with current conditions.

"For example, he said, there was a hotel tax, which did not apply to condotels, villas, tourist houses and homestays, etc. He also stressed the need to change the terms of restaurant tax..."

Source: B. Nurbianto. 2018. Hospitality Rules Need Revision: Business Becoming More Costly. *The Jakarta Post*. 10 November. https://www.thejakartapost.com/news/2018/11/09/hospitality-rules-need-revision-business-becoming-more-costly.html.

Behavioral Taxes

There is scope for higher and/or greater sharing of sumptuary taxes.[74] Like motor vehicle and fuel taxes, sumptuary taxes should be received directly or indirectly by the government that incurs the expenditure required to rectify damage done by a socially undesirable activity, and that is invariably a provincial, district, or city government.

Cigarette Excise Tax

Cigarette excise tax is a provincial government piggyback tax of 10% on the amount of excises levied by the central government on cigarettes (Article 29 of Law 28/2009). This rate would increase to 15% in proposed amendments to Law 28/2009.[75]

---

[74]　Sumptuary taxes are excise or ad valorem taxes levied on goods and services that support an undesirable habit such as gambling; tobacco; unhealthy food and drinks; and most notably, alcohol.

[75]　Article 64(1)(a).

As Indonesia has the highest smoking rate in the world,[76] the costs of countering the harm to health from smoking are set to increase. A higher cigarette excise tax would be appropriate for funding these increased costs,[77] especially as the demand for cigarettes is fairly inelastic, enabling a stable revenue inflow. However, if the rate is set high enough to deter smoking, the elasticity of demand for cigarettes will increase.[78] Although this would compromise revenue flow, it would achieve the more fundamental health objective of reducing the incidence of smoking and the health-care costs associated with it, which are incurred by local governments.

Garnering more tax revenue from the cigarette excise tax is likely to have little impact on the central government's investment and economic-growth policies. A sensitivity analysis would be appropriate to ascertain the economic impact of increasing the tax rate.

A problem is how the cigarette tax is imposed. Article 27(1) of Law 28/2009 states that the *tax* subjects of cigarette excise tax are the cigarette consumers,[79] but Article 27(2) specifies that the *taxable* subjects of the cigarette excise tax are the "entrepreneurs of cigarette factories/producers" and the licensed importers of cigarettes.[80] The tax is therefore on production, not consumption, as it is imposed as excises levied on the value of factory output sold to the distributor in the cigarette supply chain. There is no relationship between the local government jurisdictions from which the tax is collected and those in which the tax subjects (smokers) are located. That defies the benefit principle of taxation. The allocation of cigarette excise-tax revenue should be to the local jurisdictions in which the consumption occurs because they will incur the health-care costs. However, the basis for tax allocation is imprecise because no accurate data exists on cigarette consumption in each region. The only data to validate the allocation of the cigarette excise tax among the provinces, cities, or districts are population estimates and estimates of smoker percentages in each locality.

Sugar and Fat Taxes

Largely echoing the rationale for cigarette taxes, some countries are beginning to introduce taxes on fatty and sugary foods, and especially on sugary drinks. As elsewhere, a growing, richer middle class in Indonesia is consuming more unhealthy food and drink.

---

[76] In 2015, 76.2% of Indonesian men, but only 3.6% of women, smoked daily. The percentage of the adult population aged 15 and over that smoke had actually increased from 31.1% in 2000 to 39.9% in 2015. Indonesia was one of only two countries among the 43 surveyed by the OECD that experienced more smoking during that period. OECD. 2017. *Health at a Glance 2017: OECD Indicators*. Paris. p. 71.

[77] Indonesia's cigarette tax is 58.5% of the retail price of the most widely sold brand of cigarettes, which is below the World Health Organization's (WHO) best practice threshold level of 75%. World Health Organization. 2019. *WHO Report on the Global Tobacco Epidemic, 2019*. Geneva. p. 148. The OECD observes that Indonesia's cigarette excise tax does not appear to be particularly regressive, as "spending on tobacco and betel accounted for a lower share of the poorest households' budgets (5% for those spending less than USD48 PPP-adjusted monthly), than for households with incomes of USD119–239 PPP-adjusted (9%)" (footnote 55, p. 30).

[78] A 10% price increase reduces consumption by 5% in low- and middle-income countries. See: footnote 77, p. 106.

[79] In Article 1(44) of Law 28/2009, "tax subjects" refers to taxable private persons.

[80] In Article 1(45) of Law 28/2009, "taxable subjects" refers to private persons or entities from which a tax is collected.

Like the negative externalities associated with smoking, the health-care costs of unhealthy diets fall to the local governments. Although the Fiscal Policy Agency in the Ministry of Finance (MOF) has conducted a study on a possible sugar tax, policy makers need to assess the options for local governments in terms of how to levy sugar and/or fat taxes, ideally at the point of final consumption, and to consider the centrally determined rate and base parameters if these taxes are to proceed within the framework of local-source tax revenue generation. An alternative, second-best option would be a uniform central tax subject to allocation rules.

Environmental Taxes

Indonesia faces considerable environmental challenges. Its inland water and air pollution is probably the best example of a local problem that requires a local solution. Yet, environmental taxes have so far barely appeared on the national taxation landscape,[81] and have not been considered at all by the local governments that foot the bill.[82]

Some provisions of Law 28/2009 acknowledge the need to consider environmental impacts when assessing taxes on the tax objects. These provisions are as follows:

(i)   Articles 5(1)(b), 5(3), and 11 determine the basis for the annual motor vehicle tax and for the tax on the transfer of motor vehicles, and they require a weighting that reflects road damage and/or environmental pollution from the use of motor vehicles. However, these provisions have not been effectively used to manage road congestion and the associated pollution. Provincial governments, which impose motor vehicle taxes, either do not adjust the rates for vehicle characteristics or they bluntly apply the 1.3 multiplier for all trucks, as prescribed in Government Regulation No. 101 of 2014 on hazardous waste management. While it may not be practical for each province to produce detailed tables with adjustment coefficients for each make and model of vehicle, this is something that can be addressed in guidelines issued by the Ministry of Home Affairs (MOHA).

(ii)   Article 21(2) offers an exemption from the surface water tax for water taken for basic household use, irrigation, and aquaculture, with due observance of requirements for preserving the environment; and Articles 23(2)(g) and 69(2)(g) state that surface water and groundwater must be valued considering, among other things, damage to the environment caused by their extraction.

In one respect, the motor vehicle tax currently operates in the opposite direction. Article 5 of Law 28/2009 provides that one factor for calculating the motor vehicle tax is the sale value of a vehicle,[83] determined by its market price in the first week of December each year.[84] As the market value of a motor vehicle depreciates from year to year, the tax declines, thus deterring the replacement of aging vehicles with new and more fuel-efficient models. This disincentive calls for a reappraisal of the tax basis in order to better align vehicle characteristics (such as power source, engine capacity, and emissions) with vehicles' contributions to air pollution.

---

81   An environment tax was proposed in 2009. The discussion at that time focused on the tax base. Since there were difficulties in measuring pollution levels across regions, the amount of a company's turnover was finally proposed as the tax base. However, companies opposed this idea, and the tax was never implemented.

82   The OECD reports that environmentally related tax revenue equals less than 1.0% of Indonesia's GDP, compared with an average of 2.3% across all economies (footnote 52, p. 31).

83   Articles 5(1)(a) and (2).

84   Articles 5(4) and (6).

Similarly, Article 11 of Law 28/2009 specifies that the tax on the transfer of motor vehicle ownership should be determined by its sale value. Again, as the sales value declines over time, so does the tax, incentivizing trade in older vehicles and keeping them on the road. Policy makers need to consider introducing other factors for calculation that would encourage the purchase of new vehicles, and the scrapping of old ones.

With the environment riding high on the international political agenda, it is timely for Indonesian tax policy makers in both the central and local governments to consider how local governments could increase their local-source revenue while simultaneously inducing behavioral change that would favor a cleaner environment. As pollution is unevenly distributed across Indonesia, and each local government covers the expense of solving its own pollution problems, local governments, rather than the central government, should have the right to enact environmental taxes commensurate with their expenditure needs. Again, taxation rights should be formulated within a broad framework determined by the central government in consultation with the local governments.

The scope for introducing and increasing environmental taxes by local governments, and introducing further exemptions for environmentally friendly tax objects beyond the existing provisions in Law 28/2009, include

(i)   increasing the maximum tax rates on

    a.   motor vehicle fuel,

    b.   surface water,

    c.   groundwater, and

    d.   parking services;

(ii)   introducing taxes on

    a.   nonrecyclable plastics, particularly plastic bags;[85]

    b.   pesticides and other environmentally unfriendly chemicals;

    c.   tires;

    d.   deforestation by fire, with taxes and charges based on the land area; and

    e.   advertising billboards;[86]

(iii) introducing charges using the polluter-pays principle, such as for wastewater disposal; and

(iv)   taking advantage of technological developments to introduce congestion charges, such as Singapore's Electronic Road Pricing system, and driving charges based on distance, as with many toll roads.[87]

---

[85]   Plastics are a particular problem for Indonesia, which is estimated to mismanage 3.22 million tons of plastic waste each year, contributing to marine pollution and earning Indonesia approbation as the world's second-largest marine polluter. J. Jambeck et al. 2015. Plastic Waste Inputs from Land into the Ocean. *Science*. 347(6223). p. 769. In addition, the Indonesian People's Coalition for Fisheries Justice estimates that at least 1.29 million tons of plastic waste are dumped into Indonesia's rivers annually. *The Jakarta Post*. 2018. Govt Drafts Plastic Bag Tax Regulation for 2019. 24 August. https://www. thejakartapost.com/news/2018/08/24/govt-drafts-plastic-bag-tax-regulation-for-2019.html.

[86]   This could be done by increasing the current advertising tax, on the grounds that advertising billboards create visual pollution.

[87]   Also see the section on "User Charges."

Betterment Taxes and Local Franchise Fees

Lastly, policy makers should consider more a widespread use by local governments of betterment taxes and local franchise fees. A betterment tax is a compulsory charge levied on specific properties to defray all or part of the cost of a publicly funded improvement that primarily benefits the properties, beyond the general benefits received by a community as a whole. Examples are footpaths, lighting, additional road construction, and water supply and sewerage infrastructure. The owners of the properties use these public facilities at a higher rate than the general public. Alternatively, as property value closely tracks the benefits received from public services on or near the property, property NJOPs should adequately reflect those benefits, and the property owners should pay for them through a higher PBB-P2. A successful implementation of this approach will depend on credible, up-to-date property valuations (Chapter 3).

Franchise fees are another form of local-source revenue underused by local governments. They compensate a local government for the use by other parties of its infrastructure, such as fees paid by utility companies to lay pipelines and wires under public roads and bridges. They are, in effect, rental payments for the use of local government assets. External assistance for determining these fees would likely be appropriate for most local governments in Indonesia. These taxes are particularly apposite given improvements to infrastructure currently being undertaken by both the central government and local governments.

User Charges

Public goods and services are those that a person can consume without inhibiting another person from consuming them as well, such as traffic lights and security services at public venues. Users of these goods and services cannot normally be charged for their specific use of them. Their cost is, therefore, financed from general tax revenue. By contrast, the consumption of "commercial" goods and services supplied by a local government are, in principle, no different from those supplied by private businesses. Private goods and services supplied by a local government include water supply, waste collection, the issuance of building and other permits for a specific regulated activity to an individual applicant, and the provision of parking spaces on local government-owned land. Although not strictly a tax matter, the application of the benefit principle is most obvious in these cases. The cost of supplying these goods and services can be financed from fees or charges, typically called "user charges," imposed on the person who consumes the good or service. Given the similarity of these goods and services with those supplied by the private sector, the charges aim for cost recovery, including a return on investment.

User charges effectively ensure the efficient use of a local government's limited resources. If its private goods and services are provided free and funded from general tax revenue, people will be encouraged to consume more than they need, resulting in the local government producing more than the community needs. That is an inefficient use of local government resources. If a charge is imposed by the local government, consumers become aware of the true cost of their consumption. Bearing that cost or at least part of it provides an incentive for efficient consumption, thus, wasting fewer limited resources. For example, if water is supplied free to consumers, the cost of its supply funded from general taxation, consumers will have no incentive to limit their use of it, and they will waste that resource.

However, if the supply is metered and charged per liter used, consumers will be incentivized to control their consumption, thus, conserving the resource and reducing sewage.

Law 28/2009 provides for various user charges. Article 150 legitimizes the local governments' imposition of them: "[Public Services] Retribution [i.e., charges for public services provided by local governments]... constitutes one of the potential sources of Regional income" (Article 150[a][6]); and "[t]he costs imposed on the Region in the implementation of... permits and the costs to overcome the negative impacts of the granting of such permits are quite significant, therefore it is appropriate to fund the aforementioned from the permits charges" (Article 150[c][3]). However, a local government cannot implement user charges that are contrary to central government policies (Article 156[a][5]).

Article 108(1) of Law 28/2009 places user charges into three broad categories, as follows:

(i)   charges for public services ("public services retribution") provided by a local government in the public interest that private persons or entities can enjoy, such as health and medical services, garbage disposal, and education services;

(ii)   charges for business services ("business services retribution"), which are commercial in nature, such as the purchase of local government assets, port services, and water crossings; and

(iii)   charges for certain permits ("certain permits retribution"), such as those for building construction, selling alcoholic beverages at a certain venue, conducting a business at a certain location, and providing public transport along certain routes.

Part 6 of Law 28/2009 sets out the methods of calculating user charges. It prescribes the basis and general principles to be used for determining the amount of the charges. For example, the "level of services utilization [is] the basis for allocation of costs borne by the Regional Government in providing the concerned services" (Article 151[3]); the "formula [which is applied when service utilization is difficult to measure] should *reflect the costs borne* by the Regional Government in providing such services" (Article 151[4]); "Public Services Retribution shall be stipulated with due observance to *the costs of providing* the concerned services" (Article 152[1]); "costs as referred to in paragraph (1) shall include operational and maintenance costs, interest costs, and capital expenditure" (Article 152[2]); and "[t]he principles and targets in [the] stipulation of the Business Services Retribution tariff are based on the purpose of gaining *adequate profit*" (Article 153[1]) (emphasis added). Yet, Article 152(3) prescribes that "the... tariff is *only to cover part of the costs*," and Article 154(1) states that the principles and targets in [the] stipulation of the Certain Permits Retribution shall be based on the purpose to *cover part or all costs* in granting the concerned permits" (emphasis added). Thus, Part 6 requires revision to resolve these apparent contradictions because a local government cannot make an "adequate profit" unless it covers all of its costs.

Understanding the interrelationship and applying these rules requires an in-depth knowledge of cost accounting principles and practices. The charges must be reviewed at least once every 3 years, taking into account movements in the price index and economic development.[88] Given the capacity limitations discussed in Chapter 3, local governments need specific training to apply the rules on user charges.

---

[88]   Articles 155(1) and (2) of Law 28/2009.

This is an area in which external technical expertise is required for local governments, and one in which the DGFB could provide leadership. Knowledge products covering the calculation of user charges should be compiled and uploaded to the proposed TRAMPIL website for ready access by local governments.

The proposed amendments to Law 28/2009 largely follow the existing methodological statements concerning the calculation of user charges. But they have rationalized the activities that fall within these categories and introduced a traffic control charge,[89] which is intended to impose a cost on motorists who use certain roads at particular times.[90] This can be achieved by adopting modern technology, such as the global positioning system (GPS) or electronic road pricing, to individualize charges to motorists who use the specified roads at the specified times.[91] Implementing a traffic control charge, therefore, requires a consideration of how to fund a technology investment that will be used more effectively if integrated into the local government's core information technology structure (Chapter 3).

Finally, as local governments rationalize their operations and economize, an international trend is to contract out some of their services, such as waste collection and disposal or data management, to private operators who can realize efficiency gains. Indonesian local governments need to assess the benefits of adopting a similar approach. Again, guidance from the DGFB would be appropriate to help drive local government financial reform.

Incentivizing Local Governments to Reform Local Revenue Mobilization

Local governments need help in mobilizing local-source tax revenue. Particularly in light of the impaired commitment to reform highlighted in Chapter 3, local governments must be induced to access and apply the products and then embark on reform.

One danger to avoid is that of effectively penalizing local governments by reducing shared revenue allocations when they raise their own revenues. There is no incentive for one local government to independently seek revenue from local sources if it means reduced revenue allocations from the central government, while another makes no effort to raise local-source revenue (avoiding the political inconvenience of doing so) and receives its full share of the central government's funding allocations.[92]

---

[89]   Some require removal because they conflict with judicial decisions and subsequent laws. See Chapter 3.

[90]   See Article 104(1) of the proposed amendments to Law 28/2009.

[91]   See the section on "Environmental Taxes."

[92]   Indonesia can learn from the experiences of the Russian Federation and the People's Republic of China. It has been shown in the Russian Federation that "when own revenues of [a] city budget rise, they are on average almost entirely offset by a decrease in the shared revenues in the city budget... Changes in own revenues are crowded out by changes in shared revenues." By contrast, in the People's Republic of China, "changes in local shared revenues in many localities are independent of the changes in local own... revenues since... revenues are shared according to predetermined contracts and, therefore, [the correlation between changes in own revenue and changes in shared revenue] is closer to zero in these localities." E. V. Zhuravskaya. 2000. Incentives to Provide Local Public Goods: Fiscal Federalism, Russian Style. *Journal of Public Economics.* 76(2000). pp. 337, 355–357.

The central government's allocations to the local governments must ultimately be reduced, however, if the central government is to achieve its policy objective of requiring local governments to increasingly fund their expenditure themselves, thus, reducing the central government's own fiscal deficit.

This conflict can be circumvented in two ways:

(i)   If shared revenues are reduced when a local government raises more local-source revenue, the central government could incentivize local governments through the regional incentive fund (DID) mechanism,[93] which would provide criteria-based incentives for boosting local-source revenue, thus, enabling reductions in shared revenue allocations. Furthermore, proposed amendments to Law 33/2004 contemplate this approach by addressing regional incentive funds to reward the achievement of local government fiscal-management targets.

(ii) The central government can introduce mandatory reductions in shared revenues to a local government that fails to increase its local-source revenue. Policy makers need to develop a methodology to implement such a measure, which should then be incorporated into the central government's primary or secondary law.

Both of these measures should occur simultaneously, and they could operate in conjunction with Government Regulation No. 69 of 2010 on procedures to grant and utilize incentives for regional tax and levy collection.

The criteria for rewards under the first incentive should not only include the achievement of revenue targets, but also other factors, such as the extent of tax arrears settlement, improvements to the quality of taxpayer services, and targets for capturing new taxpayers.

A framework to allow for extensions to local government taxation rights should be developed for the short to medium term and addressed in the amendments to Law 28/2009, at least as long as the amendments languish in the National Legislation Program.

---

[93]   See Regulation 141/PMK.07/2019.

CHAPTER 5

FUTURE PATHWAYS

Progressing from the Current Position

The preceding chapters revealed the critical challenges that must be met if the full capture of potential local revenue is to become possible. These challenges are not confined to local government tax administration, however. While Chapter 3 highlighted the challenges at the local level, some affect actors outside the local governments, and this should encourage us "to consider the crosscutting nature of decentralization and the importance of a comprehensive approach" (footnote 11).

Reform of local government tax administrations can, therefore, be properly addressed only by both (i) upgrading tax administration mechanisms and systems that can be improved without effects beyond the local governments, and (ii) engaging external entities affected by reform. The reform pathway is thus a dual one, simultaneously tackling internal and external demands alike.

Meeting these challenges to tax policy formation and tax administration can best be accomplished through an integrated four-tier approach, reflecting the different levels of government (Figure 15). For local government tax administration (Tier 1), capacity development must continue as it was under the Tax Revenue Administration Modernization and Policy Improvement in Local Governments (TRAMPIL) project. To build capacity in local tax policy at Tier 2, knowledge products must continue to be developed for use by the Directorate General of Fiscal Balance (DGFB) staff. Also necessary is the extensive involvement of the DGFB in directing and overseeing the rollout of the reform program; catalyzing the dissemination of knowledge products, including technical information to local governments; and facilitating change management. At Tier 3, integration will be required between the local governments and the directorates of the Ministry of Finance (MOF), and among the directorates themselves, particularly for joint audits, information exchange, and the drafting of legislation founded on sound policy.

Figure 15: Four-Tier Progress Cone

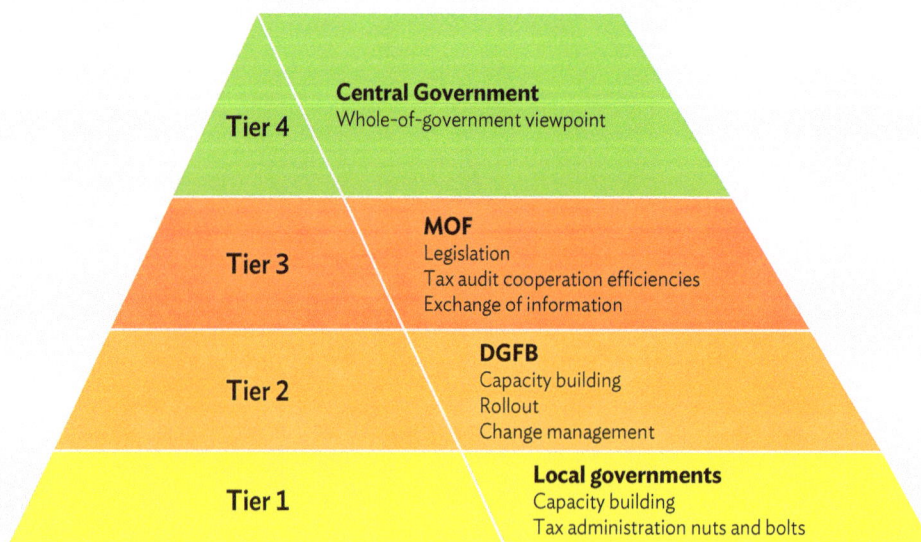

Tier 4 — **Central Government** — Whole-of-government viewpoint

Tier 3 — **MOF** — Legislation / Tax audit cooperation efficiencies / Exchange of information

Tier 2 — **DGFB** — Capacity building / Rollout / Change management

Tier 1 — **Local governments** — Capacity building / Tax administration nuts and bolts

DGFB = Directorate General of Fiscal Balance, MOF = Ministry of Finance.

Source: Asian Development Bank, Tax Revenue Administration Modernization and Policy Improvement in Local Governments project.

Finally, Tier 4 will require a pan-ministry, holistic approach to developing strategies, to ensure that local government tax reforms that affect areas of government outside local taxation are properly addressed, and that they are consistent with other policies so that Indonesia as a whole will be well served by them. Such an approach will have to achieve buy-in from the stakeholders beyond the MOF. In this framework, the actors in Tier 4 will together be a top–down force that will pressure the lower tiers into implementing reforms that will support the central government's wider policy objectives.

The proposed roles of the participants in each tier are discussed in the following sections, starting at Tier 1.

Model Local Government Tax Administration

The slow pace of reform at Tier 1 is partly because local tax administrations (LTAs) lack a clear vision of what they are expected to achieve through reform, other than the somewhat cursory edict to increase local-source revenue. More importantly, they have no idea how they are supposed to do it. TRAMPIL's work with the pilot local governments revealed a need for a simple model of tax administration to show LTAs what they should be trying to achieve, and what they need to do to reach that target. Table 6 sets out a simplified model of the baseline qualitative features of an LTA, as well as key quantitative performance measures.

Table 6: **Features and Performance Measurements of a Simplified Local Tax Administration Model**

A. Policy, IT, and Human Resource Management

1. Policy and analysis
   a. Local government tax policy development, identifying the tax base and setting rates and regulations
   b. Tax revenue analysis
   c. Field LTA officers alerting local government policy makers of weaknesses in the practical application of tax laws and regulations
   d. Gap analysis
   e. Tax intelligence
   f. Gathering and interpreting of risk-related information
   g. Scrutiny of large taxpayers, applying a variation of the 20:80 guideline
   h. User charges cost determination and price setting
   i. Selected quantitative performance measurements:
      - Annual total tax collections/Annual gross regional domestic product
      - Annual tax collections, by tax type/Annual gross national domestic product in the corresponding sector
      - Annual NJOP/Annual market value of PBB-P2 tax objects
      - Annual motor vehicle tax collected/Annual average number of registered vehicles[a]
        □ Annual number of motor vehicle transfer transactions[a]
        □ Annual value of motor vehicles transferred[a]
      - Annual amount of motor vehicle transfer tax assessed/Annual value of motor vehicles transferred[a]
        □ Annual number of BPHTB transactions
        □ Annual value of BPHTB on property transferred
      - Annual amount of BPHTB assessed/Annual value of BPHTB on property transferred
        □ Annual ranking of taxpayers and corresponding revenue collected from them, by tax type[b]

2. IT management
   a. IT utilization and development of IT plans and blueprints
   b. Business-continuity and disaster-recovery plans in the event of an IT system failure, cyber security breach, loss of taxpayer data, or natural hazard or other disaster

continued on next page

Table 6: *Continued*

A. Policy, IT, and Human Resource Management (*continued*)

3. Human resource management
   a. Function-based organizational structure
   b. Capability:
      • Assessment of the gap between existing workforce skills and competencies and operational needs
      • Skill development plan
   c. Capacity:
      • Recruitment and retention of key people
      • Succession-planning framework
   d. Cost-effective use of human resources
   e. Connection with and engagement of employees through surveys
   f. Selected quantitative performance measurements:
      • Number of employees at year-end
      • Number of employees at year-end by gender
      • Number of employees at year-end by age
      • Number of employees at year-end by years of service
      • Number of employees at year-end by job category
      • Number of employees at year-end by qualification
         □ Annual average number of employees/Annual average number of taxpayers
         □ Annual average employee salary/Average per capita regional income
      • Annual number of employees who attended training courses, seminars, and presentations
         □ Annual LTA expenditure/Annual total tax revenue collected
         □ Annual LTA expenditure/Annual regional gross domestic product

B. Accountability

1. External oversight
2. Timely performance reporting, including reporting to the Directorate General of Fiscal Balance
3. Investigation of taxpayer complaints
4. Ethical standards
5. Strategic plans
6. Taxpayer engagement
   a. Taxpayer feedback
   b. Taxpayer perception surveys
7. Selected quantitative performance measurements
   a. Annual number of complaints
   b. Annual number of whistleblower reports
   c. Annual number of complaints resolved/Annual number of complaints
   d. Annual number of whistleblower reports resolved/Annual number of whistleblower reports
   e. Annual average time taken to resolve complaints
   f. Annual average time taken to resolve whistleblower reports
   g. Annual number of taxpayer perception surveys
   h. Annual composition of administration expenditure
   i. Annual administration expenditure per Rp10,000 of taxes and levies collected

continued on next page

Table 6: *Continued*

C. Revenue Management

1. Automated tax revenue accounting systems, processed and updated daily
2. Input into local government budgeting
3. Preparation of revenue collection targets by tax type
4. Continual monitoring of tax revenue collections against revenue forecasts, by tax type
5. Monitoring growth in tax revenue collections over time, by tax type
6. Timely payment of legitimate tax refunds
7. Selected quantitative performance measurements
    a. Annual total revenue collected/Annual total budgeted revenue
    b. Annual revenue collected, by tax type/Annual budgeted revenue, by tax type

D. Taxpayer Services

1. Service delivery standards
2. Call center
3. Online taxpayer portal
4. Taxpayer charter
5. Public awareness (or public information dissemination) and education programs
6. Publication of tax regulations and announcements
7. Selected quantitative performance measurements
    a. Annual average call center response time
    b. Annual average online portal downtime
    c. Annual number of planned public awareness campaigns
    d. Annual number of planned public awareness campaigns, by tax type
    e. Annual number of public awareness campaigns undertaken
    f. Annual number of public awareness campaigns undertaken, by tax type
    g. Annual number of published regulations and announcements

E. Registration Database

1. Centralized database
2. Taxpayer registration
    a. Unique taxpayer identification number
    b. Linked associated entities and related parties
3. Tax object registration in a comprehensive fiscal cadastre
4. Interface with other IT subsystems
5. Secure online access
6. Clean inactive and erroneous records
7. Selected quantitative performance measurements
    a. Number of registered taxpayers at year-end
    b. Number of registered tax objects at year-end
    c. Annual total land area in the PBB-P2 database/Total area of local government region
    d. Number of hotels at year-end
    e. Number of restaurants at year-end
    f. Number of entertainment venues at year-end
    g. Number of parking lots at year-end
    h. Number of advertising signs at year-end
    i. Number of groundwater extraction points at year-end
    j. Number of groundwater extraction points at year-end/Number of hotels, restaurants, and entertainment venues at year-end
    k. Number of nonmetallic mineral and rock tax objects at year-end
    l. Number of swallows' nest tax objects at year-end

continued on next page

Table 6: *Continued*

F. Filing of Self-Assessment Tax Returns

1. Due dates specified
2. Information to be disclosed specified
3. Simplified record-keeping and reporting requirements
4. Pre-populated tax returns from registration database
5. Electronic filing
6. Reminders sent to taxpayers
7. Identification of taxpayers who have failed to file
8. Timely follow-up and enforcement when a return is overdue
9. Default assessments
10. Selected quantitative performance measurements
    a. On-time filing rate:
        • Annual number of returns filed on time/Annual number of expected tax returns
        • Annual number of returns filed on time, by tax type/Annual number of expected tax returns, by tax type
    b. Annual number of returns filed online/Annual number of tax returns filed
    c. Annual number of returns filed online, by tax type/Annual number of tax returns filed, by tax type

G. Official Assessments

1. Due dates set for issue of assessments
2. Timely issue of assessment notices
3. Information to be disclosed specified
4. Automatic generation of information from registration database
5. Selected quantitative performance measurements
    a. Annual number of assessments issued
    b. Annual number of assessments issued, by tax type
    c. Annual value of assessments issued
    d. Annual value of assessments issued, by tax type
    e. Annual number of assessments issued on time/Annual number of assessments issued
    f. Annual number of assessments issued on time, by tax type/Annual number of assessments issued, by tax type
    g. Annual number of official assessment payments made online/Annual number of official assessments issued
    h. Annual number of official assessment payments made online, by tax type/Annual number of official assessments issued, by tax type

H. Audits of Self-Assessment Tax Returns

1. Annual auditing plan
2. Function-based auditing
3. Auditing manual
4. Case selection focused on highest compliance risks
5. Cross-checking of third-party information
6. Interaction with the Directorate General of Taxation
7. Automated audit case management
8. Selected quantitative performance measurements
    a. Annual number of audits planned
    b. Annual number of audits completed
    c. Annual number of audits completed/Annual number of audits planned
    d. Average and median audit yields from settled audit cases, including positive, zero, and reduced assessment cases
    e. Annual tax collected as a result of audit adjustments/Annual cost of audits
    f. Annual number of audits completed with additional tax payable
    g. Annual number of audits completed with additional tax payable/Annual number of audits completed

continued on next page

Table 6: *Continued*

H. Audits of Self-Assessment Tax Returns (*continued*)

h. Annual number of audits completed without adjustments

i. Annual number of audits completed without adjustments/Annual number of audits completed

j. Annual number of audits completed with reduced assessments

k. Annual number of audits completed with reduced assessments/Annual number of audits completed

l. Average time taken for audits when no additional tax is assessed

m. Annual number of audit adjustments accepted without objection

n. Annual number of audit adjustments accepted without objection/Annual number of audits completed

I. Payment of Taxes

1. Due dates specified
2. Reminders sent to taxpayers
3. Electronic payment option
4. Identification of taxpayers who have failed to pay
5. Timely follow-up and enforcement when payment is overdue
6. Selected quantitative performance measurements
   a. Annual number of payments made by due date/Annual number of payments due
   b. Annual number of payments made by due date, by tax type/Annual number of payments due, by tax type
   c. Annual value of payments made by due date/Annual value of payments due
   d. Annual value of payments made by due date, by tax type/Annual value of payments due, by tax type
   e. Annual number of payments made online/Annual number of payments due
   f. Annual number of payments made online, by tax type/Annual number of payments due, by tax type

J. Collection and Recovery of Taxes

1. Effective debt recovery powers
2. Dedicated collection enforcement unit
3. Management of tax arrears
4. Established procedure for writing off uncollectible arrears
5. Selected quantitative performance measurements
   a. Total tax arrears at year-end/Annual tax revenue collections
   b. Tax arrears at year-end, by tax type/Annual tax revenue collections, by tax type
   c. Collectible tax arrears at year-end/Annual total tax revenue collections
   d. Collectible tax arrears at year-end, by tax type/Annual tax revenue collections, by tax type
   e. Tax arrears more than 12 months old at year-end/Total tax arrears at year-end
   f. Tax arrears more than 12 months old at year-end, by tax type/Tax arrears at year-end, by tax type
   g. Annual amount of tax arrears written off
   h. Annual amount of tax arrears written off, by tax type
   i. Annual number of recovery notices issued by type of recovery action
   j. Annual number of recovery notices issued by type of recovery action, by tax type
   k. Annual amount of recoveries from enforcement action by type of recovery action
   l. Annual amount of recoveries from enforcement action by type of recovery action, by tax type

continued on next page

Table 6: *Continued*

K. Offenses and Penalties

1. Offenses
   a. Failure to register
   b. Late filing
   c. Late payment
   d. Noncompliance with information requests
   e. Noncompliance with audit requests
2. Realistic penalties
3. Interest on late and deferred payments
4. Interest charges and graduated penalties applied uniformly to all local taxes
5. Selected quantitative performance measurements
   a. Annual number of late filing penalties imposed
   b. Annual number of late filing penalties imposed, by tax type
   c. Annual value of late filing penalties imposed
   d. Annual value of late filing penalties imposed, by tax type
   e. Annual number of late payment penalties imposed
   f. Annual number of late payment penalties imposed, by tax type
   g. Annual value of late payment penalties imposed
   h. Annual value of late payment penalties imposed, by tax type
   i. Annual number of other penalties imposed
   j. Annual number of other penalties imposed, by tax type
   k. Annual value of other penalties imposed
   l. Annual value of other penalties imposed, by tax type
   m. Annual number of cases where interest is imposed
   n. Annual number of cases where interest is imposed, by tax type
   o. Annual value of interest imposed
   p. Annual value of interest imposed, by tax type
   q. Annual number of prosecutions for criminal offenses
   r. Annual number of successful prosecutions for criminal offenses
   s. Annual number of successful prosecutions for criminal offenses/Annual number of prosecutions for criminal offenses

L. Tax Dispute Resolution

1. Taxpayers' right to challenge an assessment or decision made by the LTA
2. Taxpayers' awareness of the right to challenge an assessment
3. Taxpayers' actual use of the dispute-resolution process
4. Independent decision-making on a challenge against an assessment
5. Timely decision-making and response to the taxpayer making the challenge
6. Uniform application across all local taxes
7. Graduated appeal mechanism
8. Suspended or partial collection of tax in dispute
9. Transparent out-of-court settlement rules
10. Selected quantitative performance measurements
    a. Annual number of objections to assessments
    b. Annual number of objections to assessments, by tax type
    c. Annual number of objections to post-audit assessments
    d. Annual number of objections to post-audit assessments, by tax type
    e. Annual number of objections to non-assessment decisions
    f. Annual number of objections to non-assessment decisions, by tax type
    g. Annual number of objections to post-audit assessments/Annual number of audits
    h. Annual number of objections to post-audit assessments, by tax type/Annual number of audits, by tax type

continued on next page

Table 6: *Continued*

L. Tax Dispute Resolution (*continued*)

    i. Annual amount of tax subject to objections

    j. Annual amount of tax subject to objections, by tax type

    k. Annual number of second- and final-stage appeals filed by taxpayers

    l. Annual number of second- and final-stage appeals filed by taxpayers/Annual number of appeals

    m. Annual amount of tax subject to second- and final-stage appeals

    n. Annual value of taxes subject to second- and final-stage appeals, by tax type

    o. Annual number of appeals finally won by taxpayers

    p. Annual number of appeals finally won by the LTA

    q. Annual number of appeals finally won by taxpayers/Annual number of second- and final-stage appeals decided

    r. Annual number of appeals finally won by the LTA/Annual number of second- and final-stage appeals decided

    s. Average time taken to settle disputes at each stage

BPHTB = duty on the acquisition of land and building rights, IT = information technology, LTA = local tax administration, NJOP = tax object sales value, PBB-P2 = urban and rural land and building tax.

[a] This is applicable to provincial governments only.

[b] The point is to identify the 20:80 threshold or an applicable variation of it.

Source: Asian Development Bank, Tax Revenue Administration Modernization and Policy Improvement in Local Governments project.

The features of the model LTA are categorized broadly under the following 12 heads: (i) tax policy, information technology, and human resource management; (ii) accountability; and (iii) revenue management for detailed operational requirements concerning (iv) taxpayer services, (v) taxpayer registration, (vi) filing tax returns, (vii) assessments, (viii) audits, (ix) the payment of taxes, (x) the collection and recovery of taxes, (xi) offenses and penalties, and (xii) tax dispute resolution. Within each of the 12 categories, the key characteristics of an optimal tax administration are listed, together with some basic quantitative measurements to be generally applied over time to determine the extent to which an LTA has aligned with the benchmarks.[94]

In addition to providing time series data that can inform management decision-making, quantitative measurements are intended to be used to set targets and gauge their achievement. For example, on the collection of taxes, an annual target ratio of

Total tax arrears at year-end/Annual tax revenue collections

may be set at no more than 10%. Having used this ratio to set the target, an LTA would ascertain after the end of the year if the target had been achieved, and would then use that information to formulate what action, if any must be taken, and to set a new target for the following year.[95]

---

[94] There are many quantitative measurements that can be adopted to assess LTA performance with regard to a particular criterion. For simplicity, the model lists only a selection of the most commonly used measures.

[95] Achieving and surpassing the target may well induce management to set an even lower percentage target for the following year.

Implicit in the model, particularly on the adoption of quantitative performance measurements, is a need for the timely reporting of data and other information to management. Informed management and policy decision-making depends on the expeditious delivery of accurate data to decision makers, especially when action may be required to rectify an adverse situation or trend. This is not always the case with Indonesia's local governments, however, as evidenced by the lax reporting of statistics to central government agencies, as observed in Chapter 4.

The model is based on international best practices and draws upon aspects of the International Monetary Fund's (IMF) Tax Administration Diagnostic Assessment Tool, adapted here for subnational taxation in Indonesia, and from the Performance Indicator Standard for Local Tax Administration (SIKAP) diagnostic tool, referred to in Chapter 3. However, because the model is designed primarily for conceptual clarification, it is no substitute for a detailed assessment by an LTA of its particular situation, which would be done by applying the SIKAP methodology. In other words, once a conceptual evaluation is obtained by examining the model, an LTA should use the SIKAP tool to assess the detailed requirements and measurements applicable to its circumstances, and then identify and implement the standards required to progress toward the ultimate objective of increasing local-source revenue.

Variance from the Model in the Pilot Local Governments

The simplified tax administration model described above encompasses the critical features of an LTA using best practices, something to which all LTAs should aspire. To get an idea of the gap between the standards prescribed in the model and existing practice, TRAMPIL tested the extent to which the four pilot local governments conformed to or deviated from indicators in the model, thus, assessing the strengths and weaknesses of the pilot local governments' tax administration systems, and estimating the magnitude of the tasks still required for them to align with the model.

TRAMPIL sent each pilot LTA a questionnaire that served as the basis for interviews with senior LTA staff, in order to determine the extent to which each pilot LTA had conformed to the model and adopted the model's performance measurements. The questionnaire is reproduced in Appendix 4. This evaluation was not an appraisal of the performance of the pilot LTAs, and did not involve any numerical scoring. In any case, the pilot LTAs did not typically have the basic numerical data needed to evaluate operational performance in any detail. Instead, TRAMPIL adopted a binary approach, eliciting clarifications only when a simple "yes" or "no" answer could not be given.

The results of this variance survey for each pilot local government are presented in Table 7, which, analogous to a traffic light, shows green for conformity with a feature in the model (a "yes" answer), red for nonconformity ("no"), and yellow for partial conformity. Variance assessment was hindered by the simplified nature of the model.

Table 7: Pilot Local Government Tax-Administration Responses
to Model Features and Performance Measures

Model Feature/Performance Measure	Pilot Local Government			
	Badung	Balikpapan	Bandung	DKI Jakarta
1. Policy, IT, and Human Resource Management				
Policy and analysis				
• Local government tax policy development, identifying the tax base and setting rates and regulations				
• Tax revenue analysis capacity				
• Field tax administration officers who can alert local policy makers about weaknesses				
• Gap analysis				
• Tax intelligence				
• Gathering and interpreting risk-related information				
• Scrutiny of large taxpayers				
• Quantitative performance measurements				
IT management				
• Development and utilization of IT plans and blueprints				
• Business-continuity and disaster-recovery plan in case of an IT system failure, cyber security breach, loss of taxpayer data, or natural hazard or other disaster				
Human resource management				
• Function-based organizational structure				
• Assessment of the gap between existing workforce skills and competencies and operational needs				
• Skill-development plan				
• Recruitment and retention of key people				
• Succession planning framework				
• Cost-effective use of human resources				
• Employee engagement surveys				
• Quantitative performance measurements				
2. Accountability				
• External oversight				
• Investigation of taxpayer complaints				
• Ethical standards				
• Whistleblower reporting mechanism				
• Strategic planning				
• Taxpayer feedback				
• Quantitative performance measurements				

continued on next page

Table 7: Continued

Model Feature/Performance Measure	Pilot Local Government			
	Badung	Balikpapan	Bandung	DKI Jakarta
3. Tax Revenue Management				
• Automated tax revenue accounting systems with at least daily updating				
• Inputs into local government budgeting				
• Preparation of revenue collection targets, by tax type				
• Continual monitoring of tax revenue collections against revenue forecasts, by tax type				
• Monitoring the growth in tax revenue collection over time, by tax type				
• Timely payment of legitimate tax refunds				
• Quantitative performance measurements				
4. Taxpayer Services				
• Service delivery standards				
• Call center				
• Online taxpayer portal				
• Taxpayer charter				
• Large-taxpayer unit				
• Public awareness (or public information) and education programs				
• Publication of tax regulations and announcements				
• Quantitative performance measurements				
5. Registration Database				
• Centralized database				
• Unique taxpayer identification number				
• Tax object registration in comprehensive fiscal cadastre				
• Interfaces among IT subsystems				
• Secure online access				
• Clearing out of inactive and erroneous records				
• Quantitative performance measurements				
6. Filing of Self-Assessment Tax Returns				
• Due dates specified				
• Simplified record-keeping and reporting requirements				
• Pre-populated tax returns from the registration database				
• Electronic filing				

continued on next page

Table 7: *Continued*

Model Feature/Performance Measure	Pilot Local Government			
	Badung	Balikpapan	Bandung	DKI Jakarta
• Reminders sent to taxpayers	orange	orange	orange	orange
• Identification of taxpayers who have failed to file	teal	teal	teal	teal
• Timely follow-up and enforcement when a return is overdue	teal	teal	teal	teal
• Default assessments	teal	teal	teal	teal
• Quantitative performance measurements	orange	orange	teal	teal
7. Official Assessments				
• Due dates for issue specified	teal	teal	teal	teal
• Automatic generation of information from the registration database	teal	teal	teal	teal
• Timely issue of assessment notices	teal	teal	teal	teal
• Quantitative performance measurements	orange	orange	teal	teal
8. Audits of Self-Assessment Tax Returns				
• Annual audit plan	orange	orange	orange	teal
• Function-based auditing	yellow	yellow	yellow	yellow
• Auditing manual	yellow	yellow	yellow	yellow
• Case selection focused on highest compliance risks	teal	yellow	teal	teal
• Cross-checks of third-party information	yellow	orange	orange	yellow
• Interaction with the Directorate General of Taxation	orange	orange	orange	orange
• Automated audit case management	orange	orange	orange	orange
• Quantitative performance measurements	orange	teal	teal	teal
9. Payment of Taxes				
• Due dates specified	teal	teal	teal	teal
• Reminders sent to taxpayers	teal	teal	orange	teal
• Electronic payment option	teal	teal	teal	teal
• Identification of citizens who failed to pay their taxes	teal	teal	teal	teal
• Timely follow-up when payment is overdue	teal	teal	teal	teal
• Quantitative performance measurements	orange	orange	teal	teal
10. Collection and Recovery of Taxes				
• Effective debt-recovery powers	teal	teal	orange	yellow
• Dedicated collection enforcement unit	teal	teal	teal	orange
• Management of tax arrears	teal	teal	teal	teal
• Write-offs of uncollectible arrears	teal	yellow	orange	yellow
• Quantitative performance measurements	orange	teal	teal	teal

continued on next page

Table 7: *Continued*

Model Feature/Performance Measure	Pilot Local Government			
	Badung	Balikpapan	Bandung	DKI Jakarta
11. Offenses and Penalties				
• Failure to register	Conformity	Conformity	Conformity	Conformity
• Late filing	Conformity	Conformity	Conformity	Conformity
• Late payment	Conformity	Conformity	Conformity	Conformity
• Noncompliance with information requests	Partial	Conformity	Conformity	Conformity
• Noncompliance with audit requests	Partial	Conformity	Conformity	Conformity
• Realistic penalties	Conformity	Conformity	Conformity	Partial
• Interest charges on late and deferred payments	Conformity	Conformity	Conformity	Conformity
• Interest charges and graduated penalties applied uniformly to all local taxes	Conformity	Partial	Nonconformity	Conformity
• Quantitative performance measurements	Conformity	Nonconformity	Nonconformity	Conformity
12. Tax Dispute Resolution				
• Taxpayer's right to challenge an assessment or decision by the local tax authority	Conformity	Conformity	Conformity	Conformity
• Taxpayer awareness of the right to challenge	Conformity	Conformity	Conformity	Partial
• Independent decision-making	Conformity	Partial	Nonconformity	Nonconformity
• Timely decision-making	Partial	Conformity	Conformity	Conformity
• Right to challenge applied uniformly across all local taxes	Conformity	Conformity	Conformity	Conformity
• Graduated appeal mechanism	Conformity	Conformity	Conformity	Conformity
• Actual use by taxpayers	Conformity	Nonconformity	Nonconformity	Nonconformity
• Suspended or partial collection of disputed tax	Nonconformity	Conformity	Conformity	Conformity
• Transparent out-of-court settlement rules	Partial	Partial	Partial	Partial
• Quantitative performance measurements	Partial	Nonconformity	Nonconformity	Nonconformity

■ = Conformity ("yes"), ■ = Partial conformity, ■ = Nonconformity ("no").

DKI = Special Capital Region, IT = information technology.

Source: ADB. 2020. TRAMPIL Reports. Unpublished.

Regarding the progress of the pilot LTAs toward the ideal results, and what remains to be done, Table 7 indicates the following:

(i)   While tax revenue capacity analysis and field officer feedback were positive, progress was generally still needed on tax gap analysis, the building of tax intelligence, and the adoption of a risk-assessment approach and quantitative performance measurements.

(ii) The pilot local governments in Balikpapan and DKI Jakarta needed to improve their information technology (IT) management and systems.

(iii) LTA staff recruitment, retention, and expansion policies were hamstrung by the fact that control of local government staffing lay outside the LTAs. Virtually all aspects of human resource development, but especially in areas requiring technical tax expertise, needed extensive improvements.

(iv) The cost-effectiveness of the staff in all of the pilot LTAs needed to be assessed to ensure the optimal allocation of staff resources.

(v) Employee quantitative-performance measures and employment-engagement surveys needed to be introduced in areas where these have not been done.

(vi) All pilot LTAs had worked under external oversight, compiled strategic plans, collected taxpayer feedback, and investigated taxpayer complaints.

(vii) Typically, the LTAs needed to adopt an enhanced explication of ethical standards, practical whistleblowing mechanisms, and related statistical performance measurements.

(viii) Revenue management and monitoring were broadly under the control of the pilot LTAs.

(ix) The timely payment of overpaid-tax refunds was constrained by the existing mechanism for disbursing local government funds, which was outside LTA purview. There should be speedy procedures for the evaluation of, and response to, legitimate refund requests.

(x) Service-delivery standards and call center services needed to be introduced or enhanced. Call centers should employ appropriately qualified LTA staff, rather than subcontracted telecom company staff, and there should be information campaigns to make the taxpaying public aware of the service.

(xi) Procedures for disseminating tax regulations and proclamations were generally well established in the pilot LTAs, as were public information programs.

(xii) Dedicated offices for large taxpayers could be established, particularly in the major cities.

(xiii) Explicit taxpayer charters were generally not published, though taxpayers may be informed of their rights and obligations at the time of registration.

(xiv) All pilots had centralized taxpayer databases in which unique taxpayer registration numbers were allocated to each taxpayer. Generally, however, more comprehensive interfacing and tax object recording was required, registration database records needed cleansing, and taxpayers needed to be given secure online access to ensure the accuracy of their data held by the LTAs.

(xv) Return information supplied to self-assessment taxpayers was generally good, backed by simple recordkeeping requirements and timely follow-ups on unfiled returns. Scope existed, however, for more electronic filing of pre-populated returns, notably in Badung and Balikpapan, and for reminders sent to taxpayers in all four pilots to file their returns by the due date. Also, greater use could be made of statistical performance measures.

(xvi) The administration of official assessments was well under control. Again, greater use could be made of statistical performance measures.

(xvii) Tax auditing could be significantly improved. Case selection emphasized high-risk taxpayers, audits were function-based, and audit manuals were used, but most pilot LTAs needed to develop annual audit plans. Wider use needed to be made of third-party information, audit performance measures, and automated case-management systems, together with greater interaction with the Directorate General of Taxation (DGT) in overlapping audit areas and with respect to information exchange.

(xviii) The administration of tax payment and collection, particularly of follow-ups on late payments, was broadly under control in the pilot LTAs, but quantitative performance measures could be applied more extensively, and more stringent debt-recovery powers and clearer debt write-off policies and procedures were needed in some cases, notably in Bandung and DKI Jakarta.

(xix) Practice varied with respect to offenses and penalties. While offenses were generally well prescribed, penalties were typically based on use-of-money interest rates, rather than incorporating punitive fines for offenses. Existing penalties were not always realistic, notably in Badung and DKI Jakarta, or they were applied indiscriminately across all tax types, notably in Balikpapan and Bandung. Moreover, the use of quantitative performance measures could be stepped up in this area.

(xx) Taxpayers in all the pilot jurisdictions had the right to challenge LTA assessments, and can appeal LTA decisions. However, taxpayers were not always aware of their rights, and appeals were typically not pursued in practice. Further, LTA decisions regarding a taxpayer's assessment challenge could involve the person making the assessment, as in Bandung and DKI Jakarta, or they may not be timely, as in Badung. The rules for negotiated settlements of tax disputes were generally opaque, and few quantitative performance measurements were adopted.

It can be reasonably assumed that variances from the model LTA, such as those observed above in the pilot LTAs, are present in other LTAs throughout Indonesia.

The results in Table 7 show that the most critical areas requiring immediate attention from local governments were more strategic policy and analysis, IT systems and management, the registration database, human resource development and management, and the auditing of self-assessment tax returns.

Minimum Common Standards

Table 7 also shows that there are many areas in which the pilot LTAs—and probably most of Indonesia's LTAs—need to improve if they are to become model tax administrations. Because the effort required to make the transition will be immense, particular areas should be prioritized. In other words, minimum common standards could be realized by focusing on the most critical elements of the model. These minimum standards need priority implementation to enable local governments to raise more appropriate levels of local-source revenue.

Table 8 identifies the minimum common standards that all LTAs should meet to ensure reasonably reliable local tax collection across the country. As these basic standards are met, local governments will need to add the other standards to realize further progress toward becoming model tax administrations. Minimum standards would only be the first step toward embracing all of the features and indicators in the model.

The implementation of these first-step minimum common standards across all of Indonesia's local governments requires that the DGFB formulate and disseminate nationwide minimum criteria to be met by the local governments to enable them to successfully impose taxes. This approach, at Tier 2 of the four-tier progress cone (Figure 15), generally maintains central government control to ensure consistent tax administration standards throughout Indonesia.

Table 8: Minimum Common Standards

A. Policy Analysis

1. Local government tax policy development
   a. Tax base identified and rates and regulations set
   b. Tax revenue analysis capacity

B. Information Technology

1. Information technology blueprints
2. Business-continuity and disaster-recovery plan

C. Organization and Human Resources

1. Function-based organizational structure
2. Assessment of the gap between existing workforce skills and competencies and operational needs
3. Succession-planning framework

D. Accountability

1. External oversight
   a. reporting to the DGFB
   b. the application of quantitative performance measurements
2. Strategic plan
3. Ethical standards

E. Revenue Management

1. Automated tax revenue accounting system
2. Input into local government budgeting
3. Preparation of revenue-collection targets, by tax type
4. Continual monitoring of tax revenue collections against revenue forecasts, by tax type

F. Taxpayer Services

1. Service delivery standards and targets set
2. Public awareness (or public information) and education programs
3. Publication of tax regulations and announcements

G. Registration Database

1. Centralization and interfacing with other information technology subsystems
2. Unique taxpayer identification numbers
3. Comprehensive tax object-based fiscal cadastre

H. Filing of Self-Assessment Tax Returns

1. Specified due dates
2. Simplified record keeping and reporting requirements
3. Pre-populated tax returns from registration database
4. Electronic filing
5. Reminders sent to taxpayers
6. Identification of taxpayers that have failed to file
7. Timely follow-up and enforcement when a return is overdue
8. Default assessments

continued on next page

Table 8: *Continued*

I. Official Assessments

1. Information automatically generated from registration database
2. Timely issue of assessment notices

J. Audits

1. Annual audit plan
2. Function-based auditing
3. Auditing manual
4. Case selection focused on highest compliance risks

K. Collection and Recovery of Taxes

1. Effective debt-recovery powers
2. Management of tax arrears
3. Write-offs of uncollectible arrears

L. Offenses and Penalties

1. Specification of offenses
2. Realistic penalties and fines for offenses
3. Interest charges on late and deferred payments, in addition to penalties and fines

M. Tax Dispute Resolution

1. Taxpayers' right to challenge an assessment or decision by the LTA
2. Independent decision-making
3. Timely decision-making
4. Uniform application of the right to challenge to all local taxes
5. Operative appeal mechanism
6. Suspended and partial collection of tax in dispute
7. Transparent out-of-court settlement rules

DGFB = Directorate General of Fiscal Balance, LTA = local tax administration.

Source: Asian Development Bank, Tax Revenue Administration Modernization and Policy Improvement in Local Governments project.

To be effective, the DGFB must monitor local government compliance with the minimum common standards and their achievement of the standards within the specified time frames. Penalties need to be imposed for failure to comply with the standards on time, by reducing general funding allocations or other means. Concurrently, to incentivize local governments to pursue tax reform with greater enthusiasm, earmarked allocations from the general and/or special allocation funds should be made to local governments that achieve the minimum standards within the target periods.

Options for Consideration

At Tier 2 of the four-tier progress cone, there are four options regarding the devolution of taxation collection to the local governments, as follows: (i) no change; (ii) complete the work in progress in the four pilot local governments; (iii) roll out reforms to all the other local governments simultaneously; or (iv) gradually roll out reforms to selected local governments, over a predetermined period.

Option 1: No change. This option means that the local governments would continue to determine their future local-source revenue-collection methods under the policies already set by the central government. One of the strengths of this option is that the initiative is taken and owned locally, in recognition of the inherent differences among regions, but it can work only if the local governments are willing to participate in the local-source revenue-generation project. This option, thus, requires confidence that the local governments are sufficiently motivated, or can be induced, to seek out revenue-raising opportunities independently. The pilot local governments exhibited different degrees of commitment to tax reform, however, and even within a single LTA, commitment varied with changes in personnel.

The experience with the pilot local governments in the Tax Revenue Administration Modernization and Policy Improvement in Local Governments (TRAMPIL) project suggests that progress would be slow if it were left to the local governments to implement reforms without any inducements or penalties. Follow-up by the DGFB would be needed. If the local governments are not spurred to undertake tax reforms applicable to their individual circumstances, no progress will be made and the status quo will continue, with the local governments relying on transfers from the central government thereby undermining the central government's policy of devolving local government financing.

Option 2: Complete the job in pilot local tax administrations. This option puts the focus on ironing out problems identified by TRAMPIL in the pilot local governments before holding them up as examples for other local governments to emulate. In practice, this would mean intensifying and perfecting the work undertaken to date to enhance the pilots' fiscal cadastres by refining the property valuation methodology, establishing integrated core IT systems, and improving tax-collection mechanisms and operations.

This option would require the commitment of additional physical and financial resources to achieve comprehensive taxation coverage. This raises the question of what would be the source of those resources. As noted in Chapter 3, DKI Jakarta and Balikpapan are independently funding the expansion of their fiscal cadastre databases.

A crucial hurdle for this option is the time it would take for the pilot LTAs to complete their reform programs before the general rollout. In the meantime, the other local governments could carry out comprehensive Performance Indicator Standard for Local Tax Administration (SIKAP) assessments of their LTAs, but they would be able to do little more until the pilots were fit to serve as models.

Option 3: Roll out reforms to all the other local governments simultaneously. The pilot local governments have already increased their tax revenues, even without meticulous databases or the still-needed improvements in tax-administration structures and procedures. Although reform of the other local governments would be rough and ready to begin with, they should therefore be able to move the process along and capture some additional revenue, which could be increased over time with further improvements in the LTAs.

The disadvantage of this option is the magnitude of the task. The DGFB would need to manage and monitor improvement programs in 542 local governments at the same time.

Option 4: Roll out reforms to selected local governments gradually, over a predetermined period. This option has the same benefits as option 3, but with the added advantage that the rollouts would be undertaken in a controllable manner. How this is done would depend on two main interrelated factors: (i) the time over which all local governments are expected to embrace extensive local-source revenue generation; and (ii) the DGFB's capacity to resource a management, advisory, and monitoring program to buttress the local governments' pursuit of a greater collection of local-source revenue.

With respect to these two factors, the basic arithmetic speaks for itself. If, in a staggered rollout, all local governments were expected to embrace local-source revenue collection thoroughly within 10 years, for example, the rollout would require the participation of 54 new LTAs per year. If, in the first year, each DGFB staff member monitored nine of those LTAs, six staff members would be required during that period. If the additional local-source revenue collection in each LTA is expected to take an average of 3 years before plateauing, a further six staff members would be required in the second year, and a further six in the third year, totaling 18 staff members by the third year. The number of staff members would vary if different assumptions were made about the number of local governments that are expected to produce local-source tax revenue in accordance with the devolution policy, the deadline by which those local governments would be expected to start independently generating local-source revenue to a predetermined extent, the number of LTAs that each DGFB officer would oversee, and the average time that the additional local-source revenue generation in these LTAs would be expected to take. The success of this approach would also depend on the continuity of DGFB staff in the relevant roles, and the adequacy of the mechanisms for transferring institutional knowledge when DGFB staff positions are rotated. This point highlights the need for the involvement of the Ministry of Home Affairs (MOHA) in modifying the arrangements for civil service staff deployment.

Implementation Steps

If the rollout option is selected, it will need a structured and disciplined approach to implementation. Developing such an approach would require the following three broad steps:

Step 1: Identify local governments. Select those that are ready to implement tax reform. The TRAMPIL pilot scheme offers only limited guidance. One difficulty with the scheme was that there were only four pilot local governments participating, and they were not necessarily representative of Indonesia's 542 local governments; in fact, DKI Jakarta was a clear outlier. In a staggered rollout, the next tier of candidates for reform should better represent the local governments as a whole, so as to better inform the reform process for the rest of the country.

The next phase should not be mistaken for another pilot program. It would be a rollout, not an exercise to determine the future direction of tax reform. If the rollout option were adopted, it should be executed with the understanding that pilot outcomes have already been assessed and used to inform decisions going forward.

When selecting local governments for reform, criteria should be established for determining which local governments would qualify as participants in a progressive rollout, as follows:[96]

(i) The first criterion is the capacity of a local government to generate significant local-source revenue, given its economic base. At the outset, it should be assessed if all the local governments will ultimately be included in the tax-revenue devolution, or if some, because of their economic and social conditions, should not be expected to make the grade in the short to medium term, but instead to remain largely dependent on central government transfers. The latter group of local governments would be excluded from the rollout. Alternatively, in light of the international norm of having most local governments rely on property taxes, Indonesian policy makers may wish to consider a requirement that all local governments must impose property taxes once they achieve the minimum capacity to do so. Such a policy would prevent interregional tax competition.

(ii) Another criterion is the commitment and strength of the local government and LTA leadership, including their willingness to establish a transformation-governance structure, a dedicated team to manage reform, a steering committee or board to provide guidance and remove bottlenecks, and a willingness to work with the central government to achieve the reform objectives.

(iii) Selected local governments should have detailed reform strategies covering the short, medium, and long terms.

(iv) Finally, the last criterion is the extent to which the local government is currently raising local-source revenue, with a view to selecting local governments with low uptake.

Step 2: Formulate improvement plans. Once the local governments have been selected, they need to compile a formal, coherent, prioritized, and appropriately sequenced plan to improve tax administration, one that specifies the priorities, milestones, and the actions that would be taken to achieve the plan's objectives. Here, emphasis should be placed first on capacity building, and then on initiating operational development. This should not require the local governments to embark on many programs; instead, they would be expected to prioritize a few fundamental programs that could be realized within perhaps 2 years, such as adopting an integrated fiscal cadastre, improving its valuation methodology, and training core tax personnel. This realistic approach would mitigate regional inequalities, reduce the risk of a service delivery collapse, and overcomes resistance to the devolution agenda arising from a perceived or real inability to handle it.

To start, a local government should apply the SIKAP diagnostic tool to analyze its capacity and resources, including its need for central government funding, especially if it is less well off, to realize its local-source tax revenue potential. From there, a tax-reform implementation team under the local government should devise strategies and an implementation plan with measures to garner the additional revenue, be they administrative improvements or new sources of revenue. Although this plan would include local-source revenue targets, equally important would be nonmonetary achievements, such as planning the integration of the IT system or establishing realistic service delivery targets.

---

[96] Government of Indonesia, Tax Administration Diagnostic Assessment Tool (TADAT) Secretariat. 2019. *Tax Administration Diagnostic Assessment Tool—Field Guide*. Jakarta: TADAT Secretariat. p. 18. https://www.tadat.org/assets/files/TADAT%20 Field%20Guide%202019%20-%20English.pdf.

Step 3: Establish a timetable. Once an improvement plan is agreed upon, each local government must construct a rollout timetable specifying the dates by which the milestones must be achieved, and they must monitor the local governments' adherence to it. Failure to achieve the specified outputs within the established time frame would potentially subject a local government to penalties, as mentioned earlier. Conversely, local governments should be rewarded financially by the central government if they exceed performance targets—the higher the surplus or the more quickly achieved, the greater the reward.

Cross-Ministry Coordination

The preceding sections of this chapter addressed the strengthening of local government engagement in local-source revenue generation. Still lacking in the local government tax reform agenda is a coordinated macro strategy for the central government. Reform emanates, after all, from the central government in a unitary state and must stay within the parameters of the central government's growth-oriented economic agenda. The central government would, therefore, be expected to have a well-thought-out strategy for ensuring that reform is successfully implemented. This is what Tier 4 of the four-tier progress cone is intended to supply.

The local government tax reform program involves more than local governments and the Ministry of Finance (MOF). Changes required in the local governments to facilitate greater taxation independence will have ramifications for other central government ministries. Local government tax-related changes must either conform with other ministry policies or be justified as exceptions.

Reform affects a number of ministries, as demonstrated by the combined need to build capacity in LTA employees, nurture their commitment to reform, and keep the frequent staff transfers from undermining the process. Addressing these civil service labor matters would require MOHA involvement because the changes would affect public servants' general conditions of employment. These and other changes have legal implications involving the MOHA. For example, a motor vehicle tax would be far better implemented if aligned with the adjustments contemplated by Law 28/2009, i.e., through the regulatory framework under the purview of the MOHA.

Chapter 4 discussed the suboptimal state of data collection and compilation. There is a clear need for greater uniformity in the methods used by the local governments to collect and present data. Establishing uniformity would require the adoption of standard data reporting across all local governments.[97] Additionally, local government statistical data collected by the DGFB needs to be made compatible with the data collected by Statistics Indonesia. Chapter 4 described one instance of discrepancy between the two agencies' data sets.[98] Moreover, the timeliness of reliable data also depends on the timeliness of public sector audits.

Local government decisions on the breadth of their tax bases and the tax rates to apply in their jurisdictions may impinge on the central government's policies for promoting economic growth, so they are monitored by the MOF and MOHA. As noted in Chapter 4, this is relevant for the work of the Capital Investment Coordinating Board.

---

[97]   See Presidential Regulation No. 39 of 2019 on One Data Indonesia.

[98]   See the section titled "Reliable and Timely Reporting of Data," on p. 56.

These central government agencies need to participate in local government tax reform to ensure positive and consistent outcomes for their own policies. This will require coordination between ministries and ministry-level agencies; also, coordination requires a coordinator. One possible agent to ensure coordination to permit the smooth devolution of local government taxation would be the Coordinating Ministry for Economic Affairs (CMEA). This role would neatly dovetail with the CMEA's responsibility for coordinating subnational improvements in the ease of doing business. There should be an investigation to gauge the feasibility of the CMEA formulating and coordinating a united central government strategy for advancing local government revenue mobilization in conjunction with the other ministries. As this would require greater CMEA knowledge of the challenges of local government revenue sourcing, external technical support would have to be engaged.

An added advantage of pursuing a reform program through multiple ministries is that the united effort of the coordinating and associated ministries will signify to the local governments that the central government is serious about the reform agenda. Moreover, the collective authority of several ministries can motivate local governments to investigate, design, and implement new local-source taxation measures.

In summary, local government tax reform will have repercussions for a variety of central government bodies besides the DGFB. Their direct involvement and cooperation in reform is vital for determining both the strategy to follow and the mode of implementation. That will require coordination by an overarching body.

Capacity Building

Further capacity building is needed in a variety of areas to ensure the successful implementation of the reform agenda. It would materially contribute to the strengthening of sustainable local-source revenue enhancement by local governments, especially in the following areas of local government tax administration:

(i)   local government tax policy development;

(ii)   change management;

(iii)   fiscal cadastre updating;

(iv)   the integration of IT subsystems into one core local government IT structure;

(v)   property valuation methodology, including for public utilities;

(vi)   the establishment and evaluation of special offices for large taxpayers;

(vii)   skill development, particularly in the fields of tax auditing, including joint auditing methodology and practice;

(viii) tax arrears collection;

(ix)   cost–benefit analysis; and

(x)   the calculation of user charges.

CHAPTER 6

CONCLUSION

This report provides an overview of the technical assistance provided by the Tax Revenue Administration Modernization and Policy Improvement in Local Governments (TRAMPIL) project to the Directorate General of Fiscal Balance (DGFB) and to the four pilot local governments to advance the devolution of local government revenue generation in Indonesia. It summarizes the history of the devolution of fiscal authority, including the course of relevant legislation; provides a brief synopsis of current economic conditions and central government priorities; and describes the composition of local government revenue generation in Indonesia. The Constitution and fiscal laws emanating from it mandate regional autonomy within the macroeconomic parameters enunciated by the central government. Constitutionally sanctioned regional autonomy and the central government's macroeconomic policy framework constitute the context in which local government taxation must be addressed.

The principal law governing the raising of local-source revenue by local governments, Law 28/2009, is found wanting. Parts of it are out of date, its tax base is too narrow, and it imposes taxes in ways that are not compatible with the funding needs of local governments, required as they are to provide public goods and services. Further, a multitude of local government regulations and inconsistent tax-administration laws and practices adversely affect Indonesia's economic efficiency, create barriers to investment, and undermine cost-effective business operations. Together with the increasing maximum rates of certain taxes and a limited expansion of the tax base, the proposed amendments to Law 28/2009 offer more streamlined and coherent legislation on the imposition of local government taxes. Yet, notwithstanding the undisputed shortcomings of Law 28/2009, progress in the House of Representatives on the amendments to the law has been sluggish. This tardiness has stifled new opportunities for local governments to broaden their local-source revenue base and to facilitate a greater ease of doing business in Indonesia.

In the medium to long term, other aspects of local government taxation policy need to be examined within the national macroeconomic framework, with a view to broadening further the local-source tax revenue base, as nearly three-quarters of local governments already impose taxes on most of the bases available to them. Chapter 4 presented nine areas that merit further investigation, but the consequential policy decisions would require more reliable and timely tax collection data from the local governments.

Nonetheless, the TRAMPIL project highlighted the fact that, despite the need for further local government tax-policy development and the slow progress of legislation, local governments can still increase their revenue appreciably by upgrading their tax administration to modern international standards. Moreover, many local governments have yet to implement various taxes currently allowed under Law 28/2009.

Chapter 3 described how TRAMPIL established a solid foundation for further progress on local-source revenue mobilization in the four pilot local governments. However, it also showed that TRAMPIL's achievements with the pilot local governments did not come easily. It is unlikely that these challenges are unique to the pilots; indeed, they probably reflect wider systemic problems throughout Indonesia's 542 provincial, district, and city governments. These problems must, therefore, be addressed expeditiously if local government revenue mobilization is to continue successfully.

TRAMPIL's work with the four pilot local governments made it clear that many local tax administration (LTA) administrative mechanisms and practices are deficient. The most significant problem facing the reform agenda is a capability deficit in LTAs. Substantial improvement can come through (i) the creation of comprehensive fiscal cadastre databases for registering tax objects, especially as virtually all local governments depend on their revenue from the urban and rural land and building tax (PBB-P2); (ii) the establishment of fully integrated core information technology systems; and (iii) improved capacity. Two particular challenges are the inequality of human resource capacity among local governments, with poorer regions simply lacking the resources to attract and retain the highly skilled personnel, and the failure of human resources to reflect the diversity of Indonesia's regional economies and societies. Additional central government funding would be required to address these issues, and outsourcing options would have to be considered.

In addition, commitment to tax reform varies among the local governments, with reluctance often due to individual resistance to change. And where staff rotation is frequent, an enthusiastic official may be replaced with a less enthusiastic one.

The tax administration component of the TRAMPIL project was designed to help pilot LTAs improve their administrative systems, and to facilitate the dissemination of information about these improvements to other local governments. During its 5-year pilot-implementation phase, TRAMPIL generated considerable progress by (i) providing training and practical assistance to enhance the breadth, depth, and reliability of the pilot local governments' fiscal cadastre databases; (ii) raising the standards of their information technology systems; and (iii) improving their LTA organizational structures and business processes. These improvements ultimately resulted in increased tax collections. Further, the TRAMPIL website may have created an avenue through which technical support can be disseminated effectively from the DGFB to LTAs and among LTAs.

Capacity varies across local governments, so the pilot governments were in far different positions following the close of the TRAMPIL technical assistance phase. The extent of improvements in the quality of the LTAs was mixed. As expected, the most substantial progress occurred in the Special Capital Region (DKI) of Jakarta, chiefly because it had vastly more resources, both financial and human, than the other local governments. For that reason, DKI Jakarta is an exception, not only among the pilot local governments, but also among all of Indonesia's local governments. By contrast, the pace of reform in Balikpapan and Bandung had slowed. The TRAMPIL experience with the four pilot local governments suggests that local government tax reform will be uneven across Indonesia.

The next phase in the project to enhance local-source revenue generation will require local governments to embrace a range of reforms to overcome these impediments. This document outlined various remedies, which are embodied in a four-tier approach.

At Tier 1, the micro level, LTAs need to understand and aspire to a model local-government tax administration centered on local revenue mobilization. A simplified model presented in Chapter 5 listed the major actions for local governments to take to achieve that aspiration. The path of progression would require

(i)   the adoption of minimum common standards to

    a.   ensure operational capacity to carry out reform without undermining service delivery,

    b.   overcome tepid commitment to reform from key personnel, and

    c.   extend reasonably consistent tax-administration standards across Indonesia; and

(ii)   further technical assistance to be extended to other local governments, like that supplied by TRAMPIL to the pilot local governments, but also intended to respond to the needs identified in the TRAMPIL survey on how current practice varies from the model (Appendix 4).

If, among the Tier 2 options presented in Chapter 5, a rollout is selected, an implementation plan should be executed in accordance with the procedures described in that chapter. Managing a rollout comes under the purview of the DGFB.

Tier 2 of the integrated approach requires the DGFB to strengthen its capacity to design local government tax policy and to take a more proactive role in guiding local governments along the path to reform, which will include change management measures. It must also formulate the details of an incentive structure, and implement them, incorporating rewards and penalties for local governments according to how diligently they pursue local-source revenue, as contemplated by proposed amendments to Law 33/2004.

The four-tier progress cone encapsulates an underlying thesis of this report: the imperative of a whole-of-government vision for local government tax reform. This means that reform cannot be successfully and efficiently implemented in isolation from other connected government activities. The various arms of government must coordinate with one another where their responsibilities overlap, to capture efficiency gains that will benefit the country as a whole.

Greater coordination and cooperation within the Ministry of Finance (MOF) is contemplated by Tier 3 of the four-tier progress cone. The holistic approach to tax administration is aptly justified by the efficiency benefits gained from a cooperative and coordinated approach by government agencies auditing taxpayers with overlapping liability, i.e., involving local taxes, administered by the LTAs, and national taxes, administered by the Directorate General of Taxation (DGT). The obvious efficiency gains of such an approach would benefit the audited taxpayers, as well as both tax administrations. The impetus for genuine cooperation between the LTAs and the DGT, notably in the exchange of information, must originate in the higher echelons of the MOF to circumvent a potential fiefdom mentality at the operational level.

Tier 4 advocates interministerial coordination to ensure that changes in local taxation occur in harmony with the objectives and operations of ministries and quasi-ministries in addition to the MOF. This tier contemplates the formation of a senior interministerial coordination group, conceivably within the Coordinating Ministry for Economic Affairs (CMEA), to enable agreements among the ministries affected by local government transformations at the policy level—such as changes in staff-rotation policies to ensure the retention of institutional knowledge in specialized areas of local taxation, and compatibility with the central government's investment incentive program—and at the administrative level, such as those concerning local government data transmission and dissemination. Further, united efforts on the part of the CMEA and associated ministries offer the advantage of driving reform from the top level of the government and down to the local levels.

APPENDIX 1

PROGRESSION OF LOCAL GOVERNMENT LEGISLATION

Original Law	Amending or Replacing Law	Principal Effect of Original Law	Principal Effect of Amending or Replacing Law
Constitution of 1945 (Article 18)		Conferred wide-ranging regional autonomy on subnational governments	
	Constitutional Amendment 2000, Article 18A inserted		Established intergovernmental authority relationships
	Constitutional Amendment 2000, Article 18B inserted		Recognized uniqueness of certain regional authorities and traditional communities and their customary rights
Law No. 1 of 1945 on the position of the Regional National Committee		Established regional committees to govern local areas	
Law No. 1 of 1957 on the principles of regional government		Vitalized regional autonomy	
Law No. 5 of 1974 on governance in the regions		Fostered center-oriented relationship between central and regional governments	
Law No. 18 of 1997 on regional taxes and charges		Restricted scope of local taxes	
	Law No. 34 of 2000 on the amendment to Law 18/1997		Widened scope of local taxes
Law No. 22 of 1999 on regional government		Deconcentrated central powers and increased devolution to districts and cities	
	Law No. 32 of 2004 on local governance		Stipulated areas under the control of the central government and those under the control of subnational governments; sets out obligatory and optional tasks for local governments
	Law No. 23 of 2014 on local government		Repealed Law 32/2004 Strengthened central authority over local governments; mining, forestry, maritime affairs, and fisheries transferred to provinces

continued on next page

Continued

Original Law	Amending or Replacing Law	Principal Effect of Original Law	Principal Effect of Amending or Replacing Law
Law No. 25 of 1999 on revenue sharing between central and regional government		Sets allocations of oil and gas revenues	
	Law No. 33 of 2004 on fiscal balance between central and regional government		Sets the framework for sources of local government funding based on the allocation of responsibilities among the various levels of government
	Proposed replacement for Law 33/2004		Rectified inequalities in central funding allocations; incentivized local governments to pursue more local-source revenue generation
Law 34/2000		Districts and cities given authority to impose new taxes, subject to specified criteria	
Law 23/2014		Improved the effectiveness and efficiency of local government administration	
Law No. 36 of 2008 (Article 31C), on the fourth amendment to Law No. 7 of 1983 on income tax		Sets allocations of personal income taxes	
Law No. 25 of 2009 on public service		Services required by the government no longer subject to charges	
Law No. 28 of 2009 on local taxes and charges		Transferred certain taxes from provinces to districts and cities	
		Prohibited taxes (but not charges and fees) other than those specified in Law 28/2009	
	Proposed replacement for Law 28/2009		Expanded local government tax base, increased certain maximum tax rates, and improved the implementation of local taxes and charges

Source: Asian Development Bank, Tax Revenue Administration Modernization and Policy Improvement in Local Governments project.

APPENDIX 2

SUMMARY OF CURRENT LOCAL GOVERNMENT TAXES

Tax Type	Assessment Type	Tax Object	Tax Subject	Tax Base	Rate
Provincial					
Motor Vehicle[a]					
(1) Vehicle tax (private ownership or control)	Official	Motor vehicle	Owner or controller of motor vehicle	Successive December sales values of the vehicle weighted to reflect road damage and/or pollution of the environment as a consequence of vehicle's use	Annual rate ranges: For the first vehicle: 1%–2% Progressively, for subsequent vehicles owned: 2%–10% Public transport, ambulance, etc: 0.5%–1.0% Heavy vehicles: 0.1%–0.2%
(2) Tax on transfer of ownership of motor vehicle	Official	Transfer of ownership of motor vehicle	Transferee	Sales value of the vehicle weighted to reflect road damage and/or pollution of the environment as a consequence of using the motor vehicle	Maximum rates: General: On first transfer: 20% On subsequent transfers: 1% Heavy vehicles: On first transfer: 0.75% On subsequent transfers: 0.075%
Motor vehicle fuel tax	Self-assessment	Motor vehicle fuel	Fuel suppliers	Sales price of fuel before value-added tax	Maximum rate: 10%
Surface water tax[b]	Self-assessment	Removal and/or use of surface water	Private persons or entities that remove and/or use surface water	Acquired value of surface water	Maximum rate: 10%
Cigarette excise tax[c]	Self-assessment	Cigarette excises	Producers and importers of cigarettes	Cigarette excises	Fixed rate of cigarette excise tax: 10%

continued on next page

Continued

Tax Type	Assessment Type	Tax Object	Tax Subject	Tax Base	Rate
District or City					
Property (land and building) tax (1) PBB-P2	Official	Land and/or buildings owned, controlled, and/or used by private persons or entities, except for properties used for the business activities of plantations, forestry, and mining[d]	Private persons or entities that own rights to land and/or acquire rights to benefit from land, and/or own, control, and/or acquire rights to benefit from a building	Acquisition price,[e] minus exempt tax object value of at least Rp10 million per tax subject	Maximum rate: 0.3%
(2) Acquisition of rights to land and buildings	Official	Acquired rights to land and/or buildings	Private persons or entities acquiring rights to land and/or buildings	Acquisition price,[e] minus exempt tax-object value of at least: (i) Rp60 million per tax subject (general); and (ii) Rp300 million per tax subject (rights received by inheritance or will from private persons related by blood in a straight line, one degree upward and one degree downward, with the testator, and between husband and wife)	Maximum rate: 5%
Hotel tax	Self-assessment	Services provided by hotels for payment, including supplementary support services with the characteristics of providing ease and comfort, including sports and entertainment facilities	Private persons or entities operating hotels	Total payment or the amount that should be paid to the hotel	Maximum rate: 10%
Restaurant tax	Self-assessment	Services provided by restaurants[f]	Restaurant operators	Total payments received or that should be received by the restaurants	Maximum rate: 10%
Entertainment tax	Self-assessment	Services for organizing entertainment for which payment is collected	Private persons or entities organizing entertainment	Total amount of money received or that the organizers of entertainment should receive	Maximum rates: General: 35% Traditional arts: 10% Fashion shows, beauty contests, discotheques, karaoke, night clubs, games of skill, massage parlors, steam baths and spas: 75%

continued on next page

Continued

Tax Type	Assessment Type	Tax Object	Tax Subject	Tax Base	Rate
Advertising tax	Self-assessment	All types of advertising	Private persons or entities carrying out advertising	Rental value of the advertisement,[g] according to local government regulation	Maximum rate: 25%
Street lighting (electricity) tax[h]	Self-assessment	Use of electricity, whether self-generated (electric power generators) or acquired from other sources	Private persons or entities benefiting from electricity Suppliers of electricity	Available capacity of self-generated electricity, amount of electricity used, period of time it was used, and electricity unit price applicable within the local government jurisdiction For suppliers: sales price of electricity	Maximum rates: General: 10% Power provided by electricity suppliers and used by industries and by natural oil and gas fields: 3% Self-generated electricity: 1.5%
Tax on nonmetallic minerals and on non-rock minerals	Self-assessment	Removal of listed nonmetallic and non-rock minerals	Private persons or entities removing nonmetallic or non-rock minerals	Sales value of proceeds from removed nonmetallic and non-rock minerals	Maximum rate: 25%
Parking tax	Self-assessment	Operation of parking lots and spaces	Private persons or entities operating parking lots and spaces	Total amount of payment or the total that should be paid to the operator of parking lots and spaces	Maximum rate: 30%
Groundwater tax	Self-assessment	Extraction and/or use of groundwater	Private persons or entities that extract and/or use groundwater	Acquired value of the groundwater[i]	Maximum rate: 20%
Swallows' nest tax	Self-assessment	Removal and/or exploitation of swallows' nests	Private persons or entities that remove and/or exploit swallows' nests	Sales value of swallows' nests	Maximum rate: 10%

PBB-P2 = urban and rural land and building tax.

[a] At least 10% of the proceeds of the motor vehicle tax, including that distributed to the districts and cities, must be applied toward the development and/or maintenance of roads and the improvement of modes and facilities of public transport.

[b] Surface water is "all water available on the ground surface, excluding seawater, whether at sea or on land": Article 1(18) of Law No. 28 of 2009 on local taxes and charges.

[c] At least 50% is to be allocated to the national health insurance scheme, with the balance going to the cigarette industry, notably to improve raw materials and industry education: Minister of Finance Regulation Number 222/PMK.07/2017 on the use, monitoring, and evaluation of tobacco product profit sharing funds.

[d] Areas used for the business activities of plantations, forestry, and mining are intended to be covered by the land and building tax for mining, forestry, and plantations.

[e] The "acquisition price" of the land and buildings cannot be less than the tax object sales value in the year of acquisition.

[f] The tax is based on the minimum value of the services provided, determined according to local government regulation.

[g] This is calculated by considering the type of advertisement, material used, location of placement, time, duration of placement, and advertising medium.

[h] An unspecified portion of the street lighting tax is allocated to the supply of street lighting.

[i] This is calculated by considering the type and location of the water source, the purpose of the extraction and/or usage of the water, the volume of water removed and/or used, the quality of the water, and the damage to the environment.

Source: Asian Development Bank, Tax Revenue Administration Modernization and Policy Improvement in Local Governments project.

APPENDIX 3

ANALYSIS OF PIGGYBACKING ON THE PERSONAL INCOME TAX

The application of a personal income tax (PIT) surcharge in Indonesia is justified by its use primarily in the Nordic countries (Denmark, Finland, Iceland, Norway, and Sweden) and in Canada and Italy. This is contentious because the situation in Indonesia is far removed from that of developed countries. Since those countries rely heavily on PIT and social security contributions to fund expenditure on social welfare, they have very sophisticated tax-administration procedures to ensure high individual compliance. That is not the case in Indonesia, or in many other developing countries, where the large informal sector makes PIT problematic for the imposition of surcharges.

In Indonesia, most personal income appears to fall outside the PIT net. In 2017, just over half of all workers were informally employed, with self-employed workers accounting for 40% of all employment and 72% of self-employed workers operating in the informal sector.[1] Further, the threshold above which PIT is paid was just over double the average employee earnings in 2016, and almost three times that for taxpayers with a dependent wife and three dependent children. Thus, even individuals earning well over the average income do not pay PIT, and this substantially reducing the number of citizens paying PIT. Moreover, the highest marginal tax rate is not payable until approximately 20 times the average wage.[2] As illustrated in Figure A3.1, Indonesia consequently has the second-lowest ratio of PIT to gross domestic product (GDP) in the Southeast Asian countries surveyed, varying from 0.8% to 1.9% from 2008 to 2017, and not exceeding 1.0% since 2011.

Another weakness in using PIT as a residence-determined allocation base, or as a target for a surcharge, is that it is not comprehensive because of its

(i) exclusion of fringe benefits and employer allowances, which are instead non-deductible expenses for employers, the typical effect of which is an increase in company taxes, on which there is no piggybacking;

(ii) omission of 1.3 million small business owners, the number who opted in 2017 for the alternative 0.5% final turnover tax; and

(iii) vulnerability to tax evasion and avoidance, particularly on high incomes.

---

[1] C. Lewis. 2019. Raising More Public Revenue in Indonesia in a Growth- and Equity-Friendly Way. *OECD Economics Department Working Papers.* No. 1534. Paris: Organisation for Economic Co-operation and Development (OECD). pp. 16, 18–19. https://www.oecd.org/officialdocuments/publicdisplaydocumentpdf/?cote=ECO/WKP(2019)3&docLanguage=En. By some estimates, 93% of firms are informal (p. 18). In all, "[o]nly 20 million taxpayers were obliged to file a return in 2016. This is a small fraction of the adult population (even if some taxpayers represented two-income households rather than individuals)" (p. 19).

[2] Footnote 1. p. 18.

Figure A3.1: Ratio of Personal Income Tax to Gross Domestic Product in Southeast Asia, 2008–2017
(%)

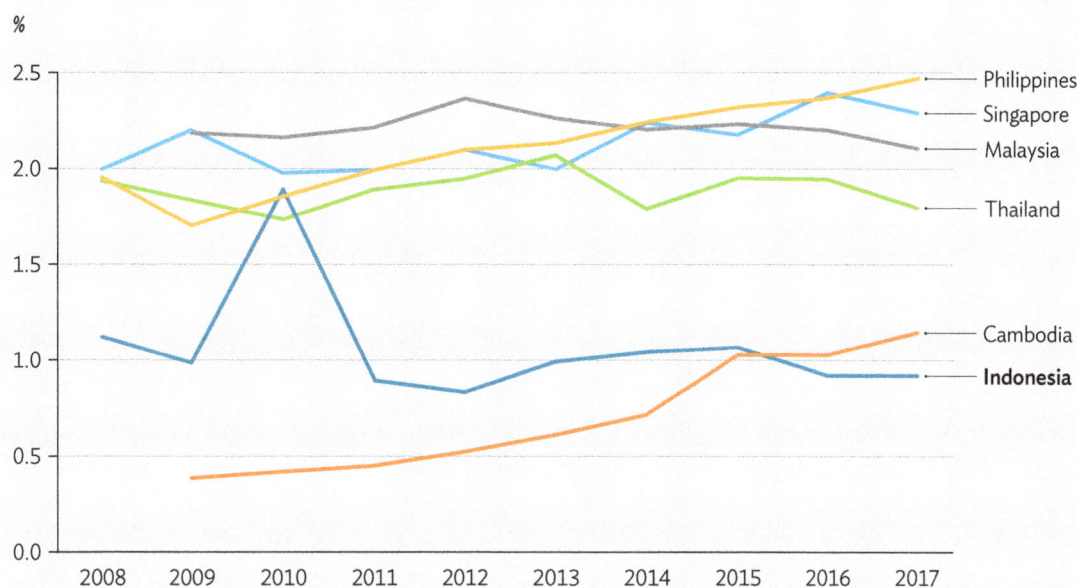

Note: Data for Brunei Darussalam and the Lao People's Democratic Republic are not available.

Sources: ADB. 2019. *Key Indicators for Asia and the Pacific 2019.* Manila. https://www.adb.org/sites/default/files/publication/521981/ki2019.pdf; Organisation for Economic Co-operation and Development (OECD). OECD.Stat. https://stats.oecd.org/ (accessed 31 October 2019).

These PIT leakages limited the collection of PIT in 2017 to Rp294.9 trillion, or only 18.8% of all central government total tax revenues.[3]

Theoretically, PIT is a surrogate measure corresponding to the benefits received by residents in a local government jurisdiction, or to revenues allocated by the central government to the locality where a taxpayer resides. A residence-based surtax generally complies with the benefit principle in that there is a correspondence between the jurisdiction from which a tax is collected and that in which the taxpayers receive benefits in the form of local services funded by the surcharge, because they are typically consumed in the local government area where the taxpayer lives. However, at the margin, where the surcharge is based on residence, individuals working outside the jurisdiction of their residence benefit from local services provided by the local government where they work—a mismatch that may not be material.

The proposed amendments to Law No. 28 of 2009 on local taxes and charges stipulate a maximum surcharge of 25%.[4] The central government would naturally be neutral regarding this rate change because it will still absorb exactly the 20% of PIT collections that it is currently required to yield to local governments under Article 31C of Law No. 7 of 1983 on income tax. For example, if the central government collects

---

[3]   This included taxes on income, profits, and capital gains of individuals. OECD. OECD.Stat. https://stats.oecd.org/ (accessed 31 October 2019).

[4]   See Article 64(1)(b) of the proposed amendments.

PIT of Rp100, it is currently required to distribute Rp20 to local governments, leaving a balance of Rp80 available for its own budget. Under the proposed amendments, the central government would collect Rp80 for itself, just as it does now, upon which the 25% surcharge (Rp20) is levied by local governments. Currently, the taxpayer still pays Rp100, the central government still receives Rp80, and local governments still receive Rp20.

Given the shortcomings of Indonesia's PIT base, piggybacking on PIT as set out in the proposed amendments to Law 28/2009 should be reconsidered. Piggybacking on national taxes is efficient, but what would be the best base for a surcharge? Subject to some modifications, a value-added tax (VAT) would appear to be a suitable choice.

In 2017, the central government collected VAT revenues of Rp480.7 trillion, or 63% more than PIT.[5] Yet, an international comparison of the ratios of taxes to GDP, illustrated in Figure A3.2,[6] indicates that Indonesia also has considerable scope for piggybacking on indirect taxes.[7] Indonesia's indirect taxes, primarily VAT and excise taxes, equaled 4.95% of the country's GDP in 2017, which was only just over 60% of the average ratio in comparable countries and blocs.

Piggybacking on the VAT has a number of advantages over piggybacking on PIT, as explained below:

(i)   A VAT surcharge would align better with the benefit principle because the services provided by the local government are likely to be more closely related to the taxes collected within that government's jurisdiction.

(ii)   The VAT base—uniformly sales revenue—is more reliable than the income-tax base, which consists partly of the gross income of employees and passive investors, and partly of the net taxable profits of self-employed business owners and operators.

(iii) The VAT is the single-largest source of central government revenue in Indonesia.

(iv)   Considerable scope exists for broadening the VAT base.

(v)   The VAT is less distortionary than the income tax.[8]

(vi)   The VAT enjoys a high rate of on-time payment, with 86% of payments made on time in 2014.[9]

(vii) The VAT has better built-in compliance mechanisms than PIT, as an audit trail would allow the checking of the output tax of one party to a transaction against the input taxes of the other party.

---

[5]   OECD. OECD.Stat. https://stats.oecd.org/ (accessed 31 October 2019).

[6]   The selection is based on data available for 2017 from neighboring and emerging economies. The OECD is included as a basis for comparison.

[7]   Figure A3.2 demonstrates a serious weakness in Indonesia's tax regime: It had the lowest ratio of total tax revenue to GDP among the selected countries in 2017, amounting to only 11.53%. Figure A3.2 also shows that there is considerable room for increasing the contribution of PIT to GDP, achievable principally by addressing the deficiencies of the current PIT regime, as discussed above. Until that is done, piggybacking on PIT will remain a flawed option.

[8]   Theoretically, the VAT is a neutral tax on businesses. In addition, a tax-neutral property tax is logically compatible with the VAT as a separate revenue source for local governments because it does not overlap conceptually with the VAT, and because property tax is a wealth tax, but the VAT is a consumption tax. Leaving aside tax neutrality, the same absence of conflict applies to PIT.

[9]   Footnote 1, p. 13.

Figure A3.2: Selected Ratios of Tax to Gross Domestic Product, 2017
(%)

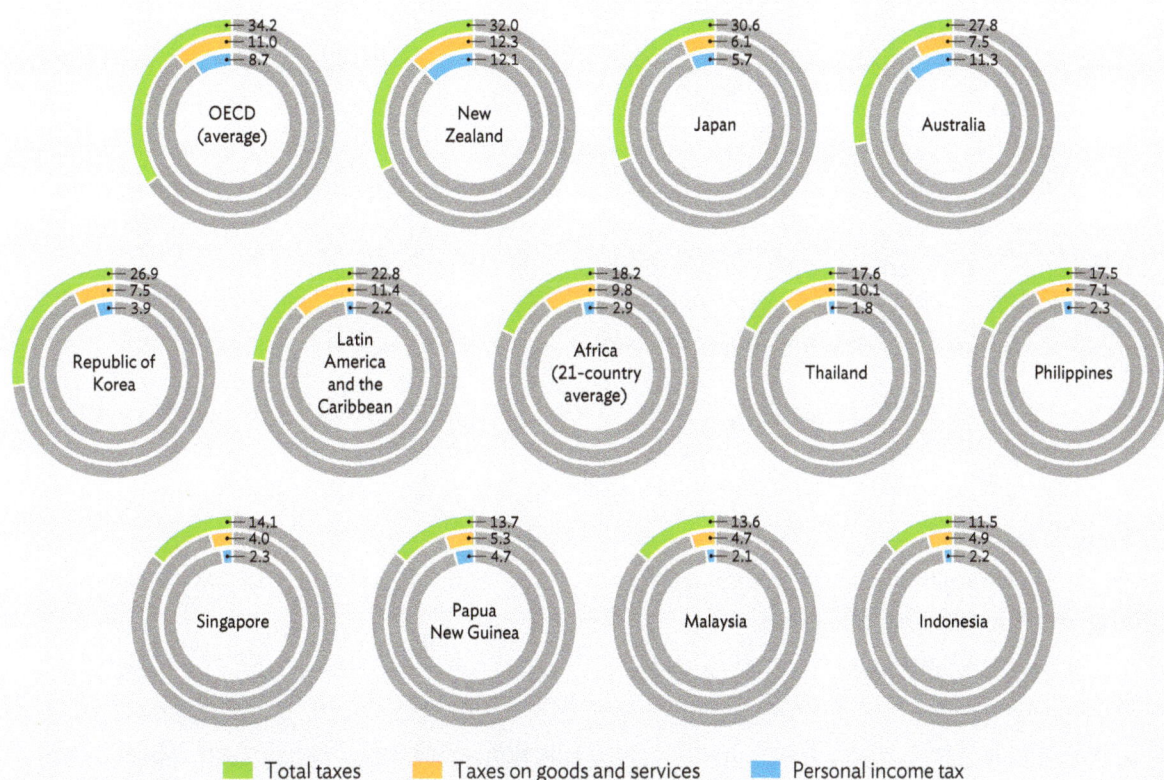

OECD (average) — 34.2, 11.0, 8.7	New Zealand — 32.0, 12.3, 12.1	Japan — 30.6, 6.1, 5.7	Australia — 27.8, 7.5, 11.3
Republic of Korea — 26.9, 7.5, 3.9	Latin America and the Caribbean — 22.8, 11.4, 2.2	Africa (21-country average) — 18.2, 9.8, 2.9	Thailand — 17.6, 10.1, 1.8	Philippines — 17.5, 7.1, 2.3
Singapore — 14.1, 4.0, 2.3	Papua New Guinea — 13.7, 5.3, 4.7	Malaysia — 13.6, 4.7, 2.1	Indonesia — 11.5, 4.9, 2.2

■ Total taxes   ■ Taxes on goods and services   ■ Personal income tax

OECD = Organisation for Economic Co-operation and Development.

Source: OECD. OECD.Stat. https://stats.oecd.org/ (accessed 31 October 2019).

(viii) As a tax on consumption, the VAT is similar to hotel, restaurant, entertainment, parking, and groundwater taxes. To enhance administrative efficiency, it could replace those taxes altogether.[10] That would prevent the cascading effect of local government taxes and, absent increased-taxpayer compliance costs, leave VAT-registered suppliers of those goods and services in a tax-neutral position.[11]

VAT revenue sharing occurs in other countries, as well. In Japan, for example, 25% of central government-imposed VAT is allocated to prefectures (equivalent to provinces), 75.0% on the basis of estimated territorial consumption, 12.5% on the number of employees, and 12.5% on the population. Prefectures are then required to allocate certain percentages of their share to municipalities, giving equal weight to the municipalities and population.

---

[10] On hotel and restaurant taxes, the OECD reports that the proceeds are modest compared with consumer spending, suggesting that compliance is low. In 2016, revenues equaled 1.2% of consumer spending on hotels and restaurants, according to national accounts data, which had barely changed from 1.1% in 2010 (footnote 1, pp. 28–29).

[11] The OECD argues that, as well as improving administrative efficiency and removing the cascading effect, merging local government self-assessment taxes into the VAT regime "may increase overall revenue through better compliance, even though VAT on inputs could be deducted" (footnote 1, p. 29).

The central government of the Republic of Korea allocates 5% of its national VAT revenue to local governments based on each region's estimated share of private final consumption. Australia and Canada also allocate their federally collected VAT to their states and provinces.

To engender administrative efficiencies and to incentivize local governments to augment VAT collection in their jurisdictions, suitably qualified auditors from the local tax administration could audit VAT returns from their areas; and the resulting additional tax revenue could be shared according to an agreed formula between the central and local governments. This is an extension of the holistic approach to central and local governance, which would again require cooperation between the Directorate General of Taxation and the local governments, as advocated in the context of local self-assessment taxes in Chapter 3.

The arguments against piggybacking on the VAT in Indonesia are as follows:

(i)   A VAT reinforces transfers of centrally collected taxes to local governments, which would contradict the central government policy of requiring local governments to increasingly source their financing from local-source revenue—an argument that applies equally to piggybacking on PIT.

(ii) A mechanism would be required to allocate the VAT revenue collected by the central government to the local governments. (However, as demonstrated by the countries referred to above, this should not be an insurmountable problem).

(iii) Identifying the source of VATs would be problematic where a VAT-registered taxpayer (a head office or the parent company of a group of companies) files one VAT return that incorporates VATs collected by branches and/or subsidiaries in various local jurisdictions. This objection can be met by requiring the filer of the consolidated return to identify, with reasonable proximity,[12] the portion of the total VAT payment that was derived from specific regions—information that would be available to the central filer because it was needed to compile the consolidated VAT return in the first place. Regulations can readily prescribe the methodology.

(iv) The extremely high current VAT threshold means that some suppliers of goods and services that now charge hotel, restaurant, entertainment, advertising, or parking taxes might not be required to register for the VAT,[13] in which case their customers would no longer have to pay a consumption tax.[14]

(v)   Compensation through the general allocation fund or other means would still be required for local governments that have relatively low VAT contributions because of their underdeveloped economies, though the compensation would be expected to decline over time as those regions develop. The same argument applies to the PIT collected from them.

---

[12] Apportionment in taxation is generally not an exact science.

[13] Indonesia's VAT registration threshold is currently Rp4.8 billion, which is the second-highest in the world, after Singapore. Quite apart from local taxation, this threshold clearly needs reviewing. The irony is that an extremely high VAT exemption threshold is adopted to relieve small businesses of the tax compliance burdens of the VAT, but small operators that are subject to local government self-assessment taxes are given no relief from the compliance burdens of those taxes—though, admittedly, complying with a VAT regime is more burdensome than complying with local government self-assessment taxes.

[14] However, because those suppliers would then be ineligible for input tax deductions, which reimburse VAT-registered suppliers for the VAT that they pay on their purchases, the cost base of the unregistered suppliers—and, therefore, their prices to the end consumers—are nevertheless increased. When coupled with cost-plus profit margins, these increases narrow the price differential between VAT-registered and unregistered suppliers. That said, the increased price charged by VAT-registered suppliers goes to the government, while that charged by suppliers outside the VAT system does not.

It would be best to consider whether or not an increase in the VAT rate from 10% would be required to render piggybacking on the VAT an adequate source of local government revenue. If the current allocation of PIT to local governments is maintained, an increase in the VAT rate would not be necessary, as only the source of that allocation would shift, from PIT to VAT collection, and the amount of VAT the central government allocated to the local governments would be compensated by the additional amount of PIT that it would then retain.

Alternatively, current local taxes on goods and services could be assimilated into the VAT regime, and local governments could apply a low-rate retail sales tax on a wider range of goods and services. Under this scenario, a maximum rate of perhaps 2% would mitigate the cascading effect discussed in Chapter 4.

Clearly, the advantages and disadvantages of piggybacking on VAT as enumerated above, and the adoption of an alternative consumption tax base, should be evaluated, including a cost–benefit analysis. This would allow an informed decision on the best way forward if piggybacking on central taxes is to be considered.

APPENDIX 4

TAX ADMINISTRATION QUESTION-AND-ANSWER SHEET FOR THE PILOT LOCAL GOVERNMENTS

Background

As part of the TRAMPIL technical assistance program to assist the mobilization of revenue in local governments in Indonesia, TRAMPIL is developing a simplified tax administration model designed to achieve sustainable growth in local government tax revenue. This model identifies the key features of 12 strategic policy and operational areas in a modern and efficient local government tax administration, based on successful international practice. The model is intended to be used by local government tax administrations in Indonesia as a design target to achieve standards in tax administration that will facilitate increased revenue flows for them.

As part of this exercise, TRAMPIL is currently surveying its four pilot local government tax administrations to find out what their current tax administration activities involve. This will inform us in a generic way what practice is common among the pilot tax administrations and which activities are not typically performed.

Objective of the Survey

The objective of the survey is to get a broad overview of the extent to which the elements of the model are currently applied in practice. The survey results will indicate how the model can be adjusted to reflect aspects that are important in the Indonesian context and areas where local tax administration can benefit most from application of relevant parts of the model. It will also enable us to consider what features of the model are likely and unlikely to be achievable in the short and medium terms. The survey is, therefore, a very general "high-level" inquiry—it is certainly **not** an assessment of performance of your tax administration.

Benefit for Pilot Tax Administrations

The benefit to the pilot local government tax administrations of participating in this survey is that it provides an opportunity for you to consider the features of a model tax administration (which are evident from the survey questions) and how they might apply to your tax administration, i.e., you will get an idea of what you are doing right according to the model and where improvements might be made to your tax administration to increase your local-source revenue.

Survey Method

We propose to conduct the survey by interview. However, the questionnaire is provided to you in advance so that you can see the types of things we are looking at and so that the right people will be available during our visit to answer the questions and to provide narratives.

To keep it simple, the questionnaire largely comprises "tick the box", Yes/No questions, with some open-ended questions to elucidate certain points. Not all questions will be relevant to your tax administration, so the questionnaire uses "Go to" directions to ensure you do not waste time on irrelevant matters.

Thank you in advance for your participation in the survey.

Local Government: ....

Number of tax administration staff: ....

Total tax revenue collected in 2018: Rp ....

Total retributions collected in 2018: Rp ....

Questions		Answers	Directions
1. Policy, IT, and human resource management			
Tax policy and analysis			
1.1	Do you have a tax policy development unit/staff with tax revenue analysis capability, which analyses the local government's tax base, tax rates and regulations, and makes recommendations for changes?	☐ Yes	Go to Question 1.2
		☐ No	Go to Question 1.6
1.2	Does this staff/unit do **gap analyses**, which compare regional economic activity statistics with tax collection statistics?	☐ Yes	Go to Question 1.3
		☐ No	
1.3	Does this staff/unit assess the **risks** of particular types of taxpayers failing to meet their tax obligations?	☐ Yes	Go to Question 1.4
		☐ No	
1.4	Does this staff/unit put special emphasis on **large taxpayers**?	☐ Yes	Go to Question 1.5
		☐ No	
1.5	Are quantitative **measurements**, such as those below, calculated as indicators of performance? $$\frac{\text{Annual total tax collections}}{\text{Annual gross regional domestic product (GRDP)}}$$ $$\frac{\text{Annual amount of BPHTB tax assessed}}{\text{Annual value of BPHTB properties transferred}}$$	☐ Yes	Go to Question 1.6
		☐ No	
1.6	Does this staff/unit or any other part of the tax administration carry out tax intelligence work (e.g., review media/internet reports of new businesses which might be liable to register and pay taxes, corporate announcements which might have tax implications)?	☐ Yes	Go to Question 1.7
		☐ No	
1.7	Do field officers **alert tax policy makers** or their superiors of weaknesses in the tax laws/regulations and tax administration which they discover in their field work?	☐ Yes	Go to Question 1.8
		☐ No	

continued on next page

Continued

	Questions	Answers	Directions
IT management			
1.8	Do you have IT utilization and development **plans, and blueprints**?	☐ Yes ☐ No	Go to Question 1.9
1.9	Do you have a **business continuity/disaster-recovery plan** in the event of an IT system failure/cyber security breach/loss of taxpayer data/natural hazard or other disaster?	☐ Yes ☐ No	Go to Question 1.10
Human resource management			
1.10	Is the tax administration organized on a **functions** basis or a **tax-type** basis?	☐ Functions ☐ Tax-type	Go to Question 1.11
1.11	Do you do an assessment of the gap between existing workforce **skills and competencies**, and the skills and competencies required by the tax administration?	☐ Yes	How often do you do the assessment? .... Go to Question 1.12
		☐ No	Go to Question 1.12
1.12	Do you have enough staff with the necessary **skills and competencies** to properly carry out the required functions of the tax administration?	☐ Yes	Go to Question 1.13
		☐ No	In which areas is there a deficiency of properly skilled and competent staff? (List in the order of areas with the greatest need) .... Go to Question 1.13
1.13	Do you have a policy for **recruitment and retention** of key staff?	☐ Yes	Has it been successful? ☐ Yes ☐ No If "No", why not? ....
		☐ No	Go to Question 1.14
1.14	Do you have a staff **succession plan**?	☐ Yes	Has it been successful? ☐ Yes ☐ No Go to Question 1.15
		☐ No	Go to Question 1.15

continued on next page

Continued

	Questions	Answers	Directions
1.15	Do you have a **skills development**/staff training program?	☐ Yes	How often are they conducted? .... Are staff required to participate? ☐ Yes　　☐ No If "No", approximately what percentage of staff attend voluntarily? ....% Go to Question 1.16
		☐ No	Go to Question 1.16
1.16	Do you conduct **employee engagement** surveys?	☐ Yes	How often are they conducted? .... Are staff required to participate? ☐ Yes　　☐ No Go to Question 1.17
		☐ No	Go to Question 1.17
1.17	Are quantitative **measurements**, such as those below, calculated as indicators of performance? Annual average number of employees <u>Annual average number of taxpayers</u> Annual salary expenditure <u>Annual administrative expenditure</u>	☐ Yes	Go to Question 2.1
		☐ No	
2. Accountability			
2.1	Is the tax administration subject to external **oversight**?	☐ Yes	Who provides the oversight? .... Go to Question 2.2
		☐ No	Go to Question 2.2
2.2	Do you have a **strategic plan**?	☐ Yes	Go to Question 2.3
		☐ No	
2.3	Are taxpayer **complaints** investigated?	☐ Yes	Who investigates the complaints? .... What is the process to resolve taxpayer complaints? ....

continued on next page

Continued

	Questions	Answers	Directions
2.3	Are taxpayer **complaints** investigated? (*Continuation*)		Do taxpayers actually lodge complaints? ☐ Yes ☐ No If "Yes", how many taxpayer complaints were lodged in 2018? .... On average, how long does it take to resolve taxpayer complaints? .... Go to Question 2.4
		☐ No	Go to Question 2.5
2.4	Do you have a **Code of Conduct**, which sets out ethical standards that staff are expected to apply?	☐ Yes	Go to Question 2.5
		☐ No	
2.5	Do you have a **whistleblower** reporting mechanism?	☐ Yes	Who investigates whistleblower reports? .... What is the process to resolve whistleblower reports? .... Are there actually whistleblowers who make reports? ☐ Yes ☐ No If "Yes", how many whistleblower reports were lodged in 2018? .... On average, approximately how long does it take to resolve the issues raised in whistleblower reports? .... Go to Question 2.6 If "No", why not? .... Go to Question 2.6
		☐ No	Go to Question 2.6

continued on next page

Continued

Questions		Answers	Directions
2.6	Do you conduct **taxpayer feedback** surveys?	☐ Yes	Go to Question 2.7
		☐ No	
2.7	Are quantitative **measurements**, such as those below, calculated as indicators of performance? $$\frac{\text{Annual number of complaints resolved}}{\text{Annual number of complaints}}$$ Annual administration expenditure per Rp10,000 collected	☐ Yes	Go to Question 3.1
		☐ No	
3. Revenue management			
3.1	Do you have an automated tax revenue **accounting system**?	☐ Yes	How often are transactions/events processed and taxpayer accounts/information updated? .... Go to Question 3.2
		☐ No	Go to Question 3.2
3.2	Does the tax administration have input into the local government's **budgeting**?	☐ Yes	Go to Question 3.3
		☐ No	
3.3	Are revenue collection **targets** prepared by tax type?	☐ Yes	Go to Question 3.4
		☐ No	
3.4	Do you **monitor tax revenue collections** against revenue forecasts by tax type?	☐ Yes	Go to Question 3.5
		☐ No	
3.5	Do you **monitor growth** in tax revenue collections over time by tax type?	☐ Yes	Over what periods do you make the comparisons? .... Go to Question 3.6
		☐ No	Go to Question 3.6
3.6	Do you pay **refunds**, which have been legitimately claimed by taxpayers (e.g., where there has been a mistake in a self-assessed tax return resulting in the taxpayer paying too much tax or there has been a numerical error in the amount of a payment)?	☐ Yes	What is the process for paying refunds? .... How long does it take to pay a refund after a taxpayer makes a claim? .... Do taxpayers actually claim refunds where they have overpaid tax? ☐ Yes ☐ No Go to Question 3.7

continued on next page

Continued

	Questions	Answers	Directions
3.6	Do you pay **refunds**, which have been legitimately claimed by taxpayers (e.g., where there has been a mistake in a self-assessed tax return resulting in the taxpayer paying too much tax or there has been a numerical error in the amount of a payment)? *(Continuation)*	☐ No	Can a taxpayer offset an earlier overpayment of tax against a future tax payment liability? ☐ Yes ☐ No If "No", what happens when a taxpayer overpays tax? .... Go to Question 3.7

3.7	Are quantitative **measurements**, such as those below, calculated as indicators of performance?
	
	    Annual total revenue collected
	    Annual total budgeted revenue
	
	    Annual revenue collected by tax type
	    Annual budgeted revenue by tax type
		☐ Yes
		
		☐ No
			Go to Question 4.1

4. Taxpayer services

	Questions	Answers	Directions
4.1	Do you apply service **delivery standards**?	☐ Yes ☐ No	Go to Question 4.2
4.2	Do you operate a **call centre**?	☐ Yes ☐ No	How many staff do you employ in the call centre? .... Go to Question 4.3 Go to Question 4.3
4.3	Do you have an online taxpayer **portal**?	☐ Yes ☐ No	Go to Question 4.4
4.4	Do you have a **Taxpayer Charter** (which sets out for taxpayers their rights and obligations)?	☐ Yes ☐ No	Go to Question 4.5
4.5	Do you have a **Large Taxpayer Unit** (which deals exclusively with large taxpayers)?	☐ Yes ☐ No	Go to Question 4.6
4.6	Do you run public awareness/education/**socialization programmes**/campaigns for taxpayers and the public?	☐ Yes ☐ No	How many did you run in 2018? .... Go to Question 4.7 Go to Question 4.7

continued on next page

Continued

	Questions	Answers	Directions
4.7	Do you **publish** tax regulations/announcements?	☐ Yes	How do you publish them? .... How many did you publish in 2018? .... Go to Question 4.8
		☐ No	Go to Question 4.8
4.8	Are quantitative **measurements**, such as those below, calculated as indicators of performance? Annual number of public awareness/socialization campaigns undertaken Annual average online portal downtime	☐ Yes ☐ No	Go to Question 5.1
5. Registration database			
5.1	Do you have an automated **centralized database**?	☐ Yes	Does it interface with other IT subsystems (e.g., returns, issuing of official assessments, payments, etc.)? ☐ Yes ☐ No Can taxpayers access the database through a web portal to obtain information about themselves and their tax position and make changes to certain data (e.g., address, contact details)? ☐ Yes ☐ No If "Yes", what measures have been taken to ensure that online access is secure? .... ☐ None Go to Question 5.2
		☐ No	Is the database maintained manually? ☐ Yes ☐ No Is the database decentralized (i.e., different databases in different tax offices)? ☐ Yes ☐ No Go to Question 5.2

continued on next page

Continued

Questions		Answers	Directions
Taxpayer registration			
5.2	Is each taxpayer given a unique **taxpayer identification number** (TIN) when the taxpayer registers?	☐ Yes	Go to Question 5.3
		☐ No	
5.3	Are associated entities and **related parties** linked in the database?	☐ Yes	Go to Question 5.4
		☐ No	
Tax object registration			
5.4	Do you have a comprehensive (i.e., complete and up-to-date) **fiscal cadastre** database?	☐ Yes	Go to Question 5.5
		☐ No	How complete is it? ...... % (approximately) Go to Question 5.5
5.5	Is the database **clean** of inactive/erroneous records?	☐ Yes	How often is the database cleansed? .... Go to Question 5.6
		☐ No	Go to Question 5.6
5.6	Are quantitative **measurements**, such as those below, calculated as indicators of performance? $\dfrac{\text{Annual total land area in the property tax database}}{\text{Total area of local government region}}$ Number of hotels at year-end Number of restaurants at year-end	☐ Yes ☐ No	Go to Question 6.1
6. Filing of self-assessment tax returns			
6.1	Are **due dates** specified for filing tax returns?	☐ Yes	Go to Question 6.2
		☐ No	
6.2	Is **information** that is to be disclosed in a tax return specified?	☐ Yes	Where is it specified? .... Go to Question 6.3
		☐ No	Go to Question 6.3
6.3	Are tax returns **pre-populated** with data from the registration database?	☐ Yes	Go to Question 6.4
		☐ No	
6.4	Are taxpayers required to keep **records** other than of sales/quantities/values on which the particular tax is assessed?	☐ Yes	Go to Question 6.5
		☐ No	

continued on next page

Continued

	Questions	Answers	Directions
6.5	Do you allow **electronic filing** of returns?	☐ Yes ☐ No	Go to Question 6.6
6.6	Are **reminders** sent to taxpayers to file their returns by the due date?	☐ Yes	How are the reminders sent (e.g., SMS messages, e-mail, letter)? .... When are the reminders sent? .... Go to Question 6.7
		☐ No	Go to Question 6.7
6.7	Do you identify **taxpayers who have failed to file** returns?	☐ Yes	What is the process that you use to identify these taxpayers? .... Go to Question 6.8
		☐ No	Go to Question 6.8
6.8	Do you issue **default assessments** when a tax return is overdue?	☐ Yes	How long after the return due date do you issue the default assessment? .... Go to Question 6.9
		☐ No	Go to Question 6.9
6.9	Are quantitative **measurements**, such as those below, calculated as indicators of performance? Annual number of returns filed on time by tax type Annual number of expected tax returns by tax type Annual number of returns filed online Annual number of tax returns filed	☐ Yes ☐ No	Go to Question 7.1

7. Official assessments

	Questions	Answers	Directions
7.1	Are **dates** specified for issuing official assessments?	☐ Yes	Are official assessments issued on time? ☐ Yes ☐ No Go to Question 7.2
		☐ No	Go to Question 7.2

continued on next page

Continued

Questions		Answers	Directions
7.2	Is **information** that is to be disclosed in an official assessment specified?	☐ Yes	Where is it specified? .... Go to Question 7.3
		☐ No	Go to Question 7.3
7.3	Are official assessments **automatically generated** from the tax administration database?	☐ Yes	Go to Question 7.4
		☐ No	
7.4	Are quantitative **measurements**, such as those below, calculated as indicators of performance? Annual number of assessments issued by tax type Annual number of assessments issued on time Annual number of assessments issued	☐ Yes	Go to Question 8.1
		☐ No	
8. Audit (of self-assessment tax returns)			
8.1	Do you develop an annual **audit plan**?	☐ Yes	Go to Question 8.2
		☐ No	
8.2	Are your audits **functions based** or do you audit only selected tax types on each audit?	☐ Yes	Go to Question 8.3
		☐ No	
8.3	Do you have an **audit manual**?	☐ Yes	Go to Question 8.4
		☐ No	
8.4	Does your audit **case selection** process focus on taxpayers with the highest compliance risks?	☐ Yes	How do you select taxpayers for audit? ....
		☐ No	Go to Question 8.5
8.5	Do you cross-check with **third-party information**?	☐ Yes	What third-party information do you cross-check? .... Go to Question 8.6
		☐ No	Go to Question 8.6

continued on next page

Continued

	Questions	Answers	Directions
8.6	Do you **interact with the Directorate General of Taxation** when you audit taxpayers?	☐ Yes	Do you liaise with DGT when you are planning audits/selecting audit cases? ☐ Yes ☐ No Do you liaise with DGT when you are conducting audits? ☐ Yes ☐ No Go to Question 8.7
		☐ No	Go to Question 8.7
8.7	Do you have an automated audit **case management** system?	☐ Yes	Go to Question 8.8
		☐ No	
8.8	Are quantitative **measurements**, such as those below, calculated as indicators of performance? $$\frac{\text{Annual number of audits completed}}{\text{Annual number of audits planned}}$$ $$\frac{\text{Annual tax collected as a result of audit adjustments}}{\text{Annual cost of audits}}$$ $$\frac{\text{Annual number of audits completed without adjustments}}{\text{Annual number of audits completed}}$$	☐ Yes	Go to Question 9.1
		☐ No	
9. Payment of taxes			
9.1	Are **due dates** specified for paying tax?	☐ Yes	Go to Question 9.2
		☐ No	
9.2	Are **reminders** sent to taxpayers to pay their tax by the due date?	☐ Yes	How are the reminders sent (e.g., SMS messages, e-mail, letter)? .... When are the reminders sent? ....
		☐ No	Go to Question 9.3
9.3	Do you allow **electronic payment** of tax?	☐ Yes	Go to Question 9.4
		☐ No	

continued on next page

Continued

		Questions	Answers	Directions
9.4		Do you identify **taxpayers who have failed to pay** tax by the due date for payment?	☐ Yes	What is the process that you use to identify these taxpayers …………………………………… …………………………………… …………………………………… …………………………………… Go to Question 9.5
			☐ No	Go to Question 9.5
9.5		Do you **follow up** taxpayers when their payments are overdue?	☐ Yes	How is this follow-up done? …………………………………… …………………………………… …………………………………… …………………………………… How long after the due date for payment do you follow up with the taxpayer? …………………………………… …………………………………… …………………………………… …………………………………… Go to Question 9.6
			☐ No	Go to Question 9.6
9.6		Are quantitative **measurements**, such as those below, calculated as indicators of performance? $\dfrac{\text{Annual number of payments made by due date}}{\text{Annual number of payments due}}$ $\dfrac{\text{Annual value of payments made by due date by tax type}}{\text{Annual value of payments due by tax type}}$	☐ Yes ☐ No	Go to Question 10.1

10. Collection and recovery of taxes

		Questions	Answers	Directions
10.1		Do you have adequate debt **recovery powers**?	☐ Yes	Go to Question 10.2
			☐ No	In what respect are your debt recovery powers inadequate? …………………………………… …………………………………… …………………………………… …………………………………… Go to Question 10.2

continued on next page

Continued

Questions		Answers	Directions
10.2	Do you have a dedicated tax collection **enforcement unit**?	☐ Yes ☐ No	Go to Question 10.3
10.3	Do you have a procedure to monitor and manage **tax arrears**?	☐ Yes	What is the procedure? .... Go to Question 10.4
		☐ No	Go to Question 10.4
10.4	Do you have a procedure for **writing off** uncollectible tax arrears?	☐ Yes	What is the procedure? .... What checks are there to ensure that debt write-offs are legitimate? .... ☐ None Go to Question 10.5
		☐ No	Do you write off uncollectible tax arrears at all? ☐ Yes ☐ No If "Yes", how are the write-offs done? .... What checks are there to ensure that debt write-offs are legitimate? .... ☐ None Go to Question 10.5

continued on next page

Continued

	Questions	Answers	Directions
10.5	Are quantitative **measurements**, such as those below, calculated as indicators of performance? $$\frac{\text{Total tax arrears at year-end}}{\text{Annual tax revenue collections}}$$ $$\frac{\text{Tax arrears more than 12 months old at year-end}}{\text{Total tax arrears at year-end}}$$	☐ Yes ☐ No	Go to Question 11.1
11. Offenses and penalties			
11.1	Are **offenses** prescribed for a taxpayer's failure to register, late filing, late payment, non-compliance with information requests, non-compliance with audit requests, etc.?	☐ Yes	Go to Question 11.2
		☐ No	Go to Question 11.3
11.2	Are there **penalties** for offenses?	☐ Yes	Are the penalties realistic, i.e., are they commensurate with the offense? ☐ Yes ☐ No If "No", how are they not realistic/ commensurate with the offense? .... Go to Question 11.3
		☐ No	Go to Question 11.3
11.3	Is **interest** payable on late/deferred payments of tax	☐ Yes ☐ No	Go to Question 11.4
11.4	Are penalties and interest charges (if applicable) **applied uniformly** across all taxes?	☐ Yes ☐ No	Go to Question 11.5
11.5	Are quantitative **measurements**, such as those below, calculated as indicators of performance? Annual number of late filing penalties imposed by tax type Annual amount of late payment penalties imposed by tax type Annual amount of other penalties imposed by tax type $$\frac{\text{Annual number of successful prosecutions for criminal offenses}}{\text{Annual number of prosecutions for criminal offenses}}$$	☐ Yes ☐ No	Go to Question 12.1
12. Tax dispute resolution			
12.1	Does a taxpayer have the **right to object** to your assessments/ decisions?	☐ Yes	Go to Question 12.2
		☐ No	Go to Question 12.8
12.2	Are taxpayers generally **aware** of the right to object?	☐ Yes ☐ No	Go to Question 12.3

continued on next page

Continued

	Questions	Answers	Directions
12.3	Do taxpayers **actually object** in practice?	☐ Yes	Go to Question 12.4
		☐ No	What stops them from objecting? .... Go to Question 12.4
12.4	Is the objection **first decided** by the tax administration?	☐ Yes	Is the person(s) deciding the objection independent from the person who raised the assessment or made the decision from which the objection arises? ☐ Yes ☐ No On average, how long does it take for a decision on an objection to be made by the tax administration? .... Go to Question 12.5
		☐ No	Who deals with the objection first? .... Go to Question 12.5
12.5	Can taxpayers **appeal** the decisions on their objections?	☐ Yes	How many stages of appeal can a taxpayer pursue? .... Where are those appeals made? .... On average, how long does it take for decisions on appeals to be made by? .... Go to Question 12.6
		☐ No	Go to Question 12.6

continued on next page

Continued

	Questions	Answers	Directions
12.6	Are taxpayer objection/appeal rights **uniform** across all tax types?	☐ Yes	Go to Question 12.7
		☐ No	How the taxpayer's objection/appeal rights differ between tax types? .... Go to Question 12.7
12.7	Is the collection of **tax in dispute suspended** until the dispute is resolved?	☐ Yes	Is the suspension full or partial? ☐ Full ☐ Partial Go to Question 12.8
		☐ No	Go to Question 12.8
12.8	Are **negotiated settlements** possible where a taxpayer challenges the amount of tax assessed?	☐ Yes	Are there transparent procedures for negotiated settlements? ☐ Yes ☐ No What safeguards exist to ensure that no tax officer benefits in a negotiated settlement? .... Go to Question 12.9
		☐ No	End of questions
12.9	Are quantitative **measurements**, such as those below, calculated as indicators of performance? Annual number of objections to assessments by tax type Annual number of objections to post-audit assessments / Annual number of audits Annual number of appeals finally won by taxpayers / Annual number of second and final stage appeals decided Annual number of appeals finally won by local tax administration / Annual number of second and final stage appeals decided Annual average time taken to settle disputes at each stage	☐ Yes ☐ No	End of questions